**Professional
English**

English
for Professional
Success

Hector Sánchez   Eric Tejeda   Norma Hernández
Arthur Frías   Isa Tirado   David Ramos

THOMSON
━━━━★━━━━ ™
HEINLE

Australia • Canada • México • Singapore • United Kingdom • United States

THOMSON

HEINLE

English for Professional Success

Héctor Sánchez, *et al*

Publisher, Global ELT: Christopher Wenger
Editorial Manager: Berta de Llano
Director of Product Development: Anita Raducanu
Director of Product Marketing: Amy Mabley
International Marketing Manager: Ian Martin
Development Editors: Martin Milner, Margarita Matte
Contributing Writers: Norma Hernández, Arthur Frías, Isa Tirado, David Ramos, Eric Tejeda
Editorial Assistant: Bridget McLaughlin

Production Editor: Chrystie Hopkins
Photo Researcher: Alejandra Camarillo
Illustrator: Ignacio (Iñaki) Ochoa Bilbao
Interior Design/Composition: Miriam Gómez Alvarado, Miguel Angel Contreras Pérez
Cover Design: Miriam Gómez Alvarado, Miguel Angel Contreras Pérez
Printer: Edwards Brothers

Cover Images: © Comstock Images / Alamy

Printed in the United States of America
    2 3 4 5 6 7 8 9 10 — 09 08 07 06

For more information contact Thomson ELT, 25 Thomson
Place, Boston, Massachusetts 02210 USA, or you can
visit our Internet site at elt.thomson.com

For permission to use material from this text or product,
submit a request online at http://www.thomsonrights.com

Any additional questions about permissions can be
submitted by email to thomsonrights@thomson.com

ISBN 13: 978-1-4130-3009-9
ISBN 10: 1-4130-3009-2

Library of Congress Control Number
2005909603

Photo Credits:
Photos.com/RF: **p. 11, p. 22, p. 29, p. 30, p. 32, p. 34, p.37, p. 39, p. 58**
IndexOpen/RF: **p. 36**
Alamy: **p. 38** ©Arcaid/Alamy, **p. 49** ©POPPERFOTO/Alamy. **All other photos:** ©Comstock Images/Alamy

Contents

To the Teacher

English for Professional Success is especially designed for university students at the intermediate level who want to use their English for international communication in professional contexts.

Objective

The purpose of this book is to empower students with the language and life skills they need to carry out their career goals. To this end it provides ample opportunities for students to build awareness and practice the language in real-life scenarios. Its integrated skills approach develops the student's self-confidence to survive and succeed in professional and social encounters within an English-speaking global community.

The **Professional English** portion of our book follows an eclectic approach to ESP language teaching, so teachers will find a wide variety of activities which will include practice in problem solving, critical thinking, and professional communication.

Content

The book has been designed with a core of 30 lessons plus additional resource sections to provide teachers and course designers with the necessary flexibility for planning a wide variety of courses.

The four skills of listening, speaking, writing, and reading are developed throughout each unit in professional contexts. Emphasis is on developing the life skills students need to deal with situations that they will encounter in the job market.

University students, regardless of their major, will immediately be motivated by the opportunity to prepare for the job market as they practice their English language skills in the following job-related scenarios.

Job hunting
How to read want ads, deal with application forms, plan and write cover letters and resumes, develop interview skills and learn what employers look for in a candidate

Relocating
Apartment hunting, deciding whether or not to look for a roommate and how to do so, handling landlords, interpreting leases, dealing with household problems.

On-the-job skills
Problem-solving, setting goals, creating action plans, decision-making, developing time-management skills, dealing with change within a company

The language of work
Learning the language of warehousing, placing orders, participating in meetings, giving formal presentations, practicing moderating skill

Using the book

Each content-based unit is divided into six two-page lessons. Each lesson is designed to present, develop, and practice a particular job-related skill. (See **Content**)

Vocabulary

The content vocabulary that might be unfamiliar to an intermediate-level student is glossed in dictionary boxes at the bottom of each lesson. Teachers may choose to focus on this vocabulary through direct presentation, or may introduce the students to the dictionary boxes and suggest they refer to them if they find that not recognizing a glossed word impedes their understanding of a given text.

Grammar

There is no direct grammar instruction in the core lessons. However a complete grammar resource has been provided at the end of the book. The grammar resources can serve as a reinforcement of the students grammar skills to be used for self-study and independent practice. Or the teacher may choose to use material in class to present and practice language skills required by the productive exercises in the different lessons.

The language elements are ordered as they would appear in a traditional grammar syllabus, but they may be referred to in any order. Each grammar presentation provides a grammar box or paradigm followed by contextual examples and a practice exercise.

Listening

Many of the workplace scenarios are presented and/or established through the listening contexts. Complete audio scripts and an audio CD have been provided for the student to allow for independent listening practice. Student access to audio scripts and CDs also provides multi-level instruction opportunities in the classroom.

On-going assessment

The five team projects found at the end of every unit as well as the one-page unit reviews at the end of the book provide ample opportunity for on-going assessment.

Unit tests are provided in the Teacher's Resource Book.

Unit 1

Preparing for challenges

The reason I'm applying is . . .

a Check ✓ the steps you would like to take to develop your career. Then explain your decisions to a partner.

☐ Take professional development courses
☐ Continue an M.A. (Master's) degree at my university
☐ Study for an M.A. abroad

☐ Get a job related to my field
☐ Study another B.A. (Bachelor's) degree
☐ Study in another country
☐ Work in another country

b Match the columns to complete the conversation.

Takeshi: Well, now that we've graduated from college, ____
Paula: But we'll ____
Takeshi: Hey! Have you heard anything ____
Paula: I have. It looks like I could be ____
Takeshi: I knew they'd accept you; you had the best grades in our class. I've decided to stay here. Last week I dropped off* my resume ____
Paula: Yes, it looks like a good job. But be prepared to answer questions ____
Takeshi: Sure. The pre-interview ____
Paula: I'm sure you're ____

a. . . . about the M.A. you applied for?

b. . . . about why they should hire you.

c. . . . we'll be taking different roads for a while.

d. . . . going to do just fine.

e. . . . is next week.

f. . . . heading* to New York City soon.

g. . . . at that American company I told you about.

h. . . . still be in touch.

drop off *v*	leave
duties *n*	obligations, responsibilities
availability *n*	free to start work
head *v*	to go to
lead *v*	to direct, to control
pushy *adj*	aggressive, too demanding of the attention and cooperation of others

c Look at the following characteristics. Which do you think an employer would consider *positive* (P) in a job interview? Which do you think an employer would consider *negative* (N)?

____ being a leader   ____ being a perfectionist

____ making decisions with your emotions   ____ being active

____ being pushy   ____ being aggressive

CD T-1 **d** Listen to Takeshi talk about his hiring test. How did he respond? Check ✓ the correct box.

Applicant's name: _Takeshi Oropeza_   **Date:** _June 4_

Check the option that expresses how decisive you are.

1. I like to lead*.

☐ Always   ☐ Sometimes   ☐ Never   ☐ Not sure

2. I care about getting things done well.

☐ Always   ☐ Sometimes   ☐ Never   ☐ Not sure

3. I am not emotional when making decisions.

☐ Always   ☐ Sometimes   ☐ Never   ☐ Not sure

4. I like to be busy all the time.

☐ Always   ☐ Sometimes   ☐ Never   ☐ Not sure

5. I could be described as pushy*.

☐ Always   ☐ Sometimes   ☐ Never   ☐ Not sure

---

e Describe yourself to your partner. Use the phrases in the box.

I always . . .
I don't think . . .
I absolutely . . .
Sometimes I . . .
I consider . . .
I'd say . . .
I prefer . . .

I don't consider myself a leader.
I prefer being told what to do all the time.
I always try to get things done well. I'd say that
I hate making mistakes. I double-check
everything before turning it in.

Lesson 2
Just applying for the M.A. is hard

a Brainstorm the things you would need in order to study for a Master's degree abroad.

Academic requirements	Personal qualifications	Other

b Read the Web page and make a list of the six things Paula will need to do in order to study a Master's degree in the U.S.

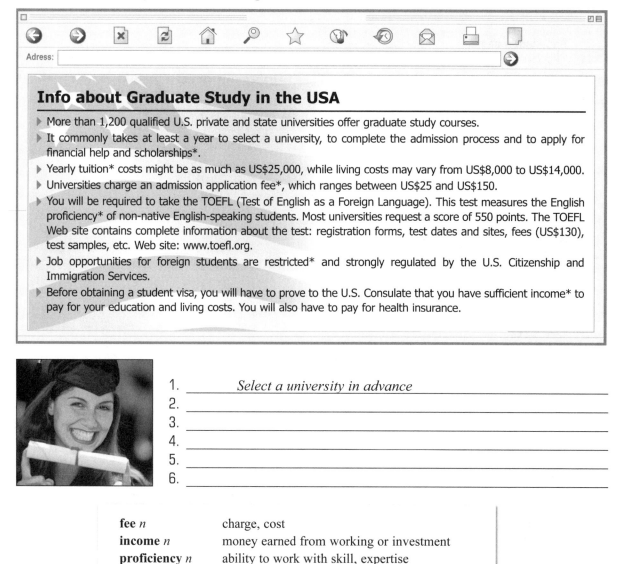

Adress:

Info about Graduate Study in the USA

▶ More than 1,200 qualified U.S. private and state universities offer graduate study courses.

▶ It commonly takes at least a year to select a university, to complete the admission process and to apply for financial help and scholarships*.

▶ Yearly tuition* costs might be as much as US$25,000, while living costs may vary from US$8,000 to US$14,000.

▶ Universities charge an admission application fee*, which ranges between US$25 and US$150.

▶ You will be required to take the TOEFL (Test of English as a Foreign Language). This test measures the English proficiency* of non-native English-speaking students. Most universities request a score of 550 points. The TOEFL Web site contains complete information about the test: registration forms, test dates and sites, fees (US$130), test samples, etc. Web site: www.toefl.org.

▶ Job opportunities for foreign students are restricted* and strongly regulated by the U.S. Citizenship and Immigration Services.

▶ Before obtaining a student visa, you will have to prove to the U.S. Consulate that you have sufficient income* to pay for your education and living costs. You will also have to pay for health insurance.

1.   *Select a university in advance*
2.
3.
4.
5.
6.

fee *n*	charge, cost
income *n*	money earned from working or investment
proficiency *n*	ability to work with skill, expertise
restricted *adj*	limited in use or in availability
scholarship *n*	a grant to pay for study
tuition *n*	school or college fees

c Read the following course descriptions. Write a FOR and AGAINST table for each of the courses and a list of additional information you would need to know to make a choice between the two.

FREEPORT COLLEGE OF BUSINESS STUDIES

Master's in Business Administration

Course structure: We recognize that each student is unique and has individual needs and interests. Therefore, we have designed a highly flexible course. After completing the core course (80 units), you can design your own course from the 30 elective options.

Course length: The course can be completed in one year, but it is possible to extend the time.

Course fee: US$ 14,000. This fee is for tuition. All transport and accommodation costs are the responsibility of the student.

Career counseling: We appreciate that a Master's Degree alone is not a guarantee of professional success. Students need to program their career around the course. We offer a comprehensive one-on-one career counseling service.

Class size: Maximum 10. Individual tutoring available on request.

NYBC MBA

NYBC is a non-profit college, partially supported by the business community, with the aim of providing high–quality training for students with limited resources. Our course fees are as low as US $8,000 and we can provide scholarships for students with a strong academic record.

Low fees are made possible by:

✔ Efficient use of staff. Courses are mainly lecture based.

✔ Fixed courses: No electives are available.

However, we can assure you that quality of the course will not be sacrificed in the name of economy. All our faculty members have a strong international reputation and many of our graduates hold important positions in the business world.

d Read the following general Graduate Admission Requirements. Then work with your partner to answer the questions.

1. **Evidence of four years tertiary study:** Official transcripts / academic records will be required from each undergraduate and / or graduate institution that you have attended.

   Do you know where to get your transcripts? How much will it cost? How long will it take?
   If you don't know, how can you find out?

2. **Supporting references or recommendations:** A minimum of two references will be required from professors or lecturers if you are applying to an academic degree program. References from your undergraduate institution and your employer(s) will be useful if you are applying to a professional program.

   Who will you ask for letters of reference? How difficult will it be to get them?

3. **Personal statement:** This can be a deciding factor in an application. Content may be either a general personal statement, or responses to very specific questions asked by the school.

   What activities will you mention in a general personal statement?
   What specific questions might a school ask?

Lesson 3
If tuition weren't so expensive . . .

a Student A asks Student B questions from the chart. Student B answers.
Then exchange roles.

Example:

A: If you wanted to buy an airline ticket, where would you get the information?

B: I would go to a travel agent.

If you wanted . . .	where would you get the information?	What would you want information about?
1. to buy an airplane ticket	*travel agent*	*prices, times, availability*
2. to get a part-time job		
3. to take the TOEFL		
4. to research graduate study		

b Paula needs a job. Read the college notice board and decide which is the best
job for Paula. Compare and justify your answer with your group.

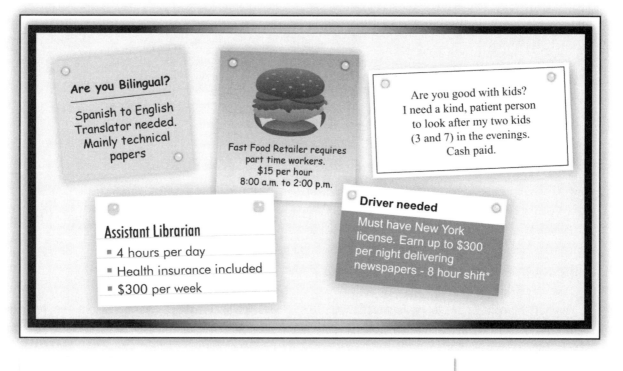

arbitrator *n*	mediator, judge
lawsuit *n*	a legal action bringing a claim to a court of law
settle *v*	to come to an agreement
shift *n*	a segment of work time

C Paula has gotten a part-time job. Read her contract and answer the questions.

Part-time Employment Agreement

Name:	Paula Fuentes
Job Title:	Assistant Librarian
Length of Contract:	3 months
Duties:	Assist librarian in organization of books; store information in the computer; and provide assistance to university students
Salary:	$300 weekly
Hours:	4 hours per day, Monday to Friday
Paid Vacation Leave:	Not applicable
Insurance Coverage:	Group health insurance plan, includes accidents at work (workman's compensation) and third party coverage
Arbitration:	Disputes will be settled* by an Arbitrator* in an Arbitration hearing, rather than via a lawsuit* in a court of law.
Attorney's fees:	In the event of any legal action taken to enforce the provisions of this contract, the prevailing party will be entitled to recover their attorney's fees from the other party.

1. Do you think working in the library will help Paula's English? Give your reasons.

_____

2. How much does Paula get paid per hour?

_____

3. Is Paula entitled to take paid leave?

_____

4. Before signing the contract, what questions do you think Paula should ask?

_____

d Change the following sentences to contrary-to-fact statements without changing the meaning.

1. She isn't stressed because she doesn't work overtime.
      She would be very stressed if she worked overtime.
2. Paula doesn't feel secure because her contract is for a short period.

_____

3. She lives far from the university so she gets up very early.

_____

4. She doesn't get the paid vacation benefit because the contract isn't for a full year.

_____

5. She will sign the contract because she agrees with everything.

_____

6. She's applying for a part-time position because she doesn't have enough time to work a full-time shift.

_____

Lesson 4

There are other options . . .

a Read the definition of Continuing Education and then match the different types of continuing education with their description.

⦂⦂⦂CONTINUING EDUCATION⦂⦂⦂

Generally speaking, continuing education can be defined as any form of education for adult learners. It often takes the form of degree credit* granting courses at a college or university, taken by full-time or part-time students and delivered by traditional lectures,* seminars, or at distance. It can also take the form of short credit or non-credit courses of a professional, vocational or personal nature delivered* by colleges, professional organizations or companies.

Types of Continuing Education	Description
____ 1. Distance courses	a. Courses that allow you to study at home without attending classes. Most courses incorporate computer conferencing, e-mail, computer-based quizzes and the use of the Internet, sometimes called online courses. They can be credit or non-credit courses.
____ 2. Full-time graduate course	b. A large meeting where a group of professionals present papers on developments in their field.
____ 3. Conferences	c. Courses where you attend a college or university. Most courses include lectures, seminars and tutorials.* For students who already have a first degree.
____ 4. Refresher courses	d. Courses where you can continue working but attend lectures or classes, in your free time. May be delivered partially at distance.
____ 5. Part-time graduate courses	e. Usually short courses intended to keep professionals up-to-date.*

b Answer *T* (true) or *F* (false). If *false*, correct the sentence.

1. Continuing Education refers to non-degree courses.   *F*
   Continuing Education refers to all types of education for adults
2. Continuing Education is for professional enrichment.   _____

   _____
3. If you wish to take a degree credit course, you must attend lectures and seminars.   _____

   _____
4. There are credit and non-credit distance education courses.   _____

   _____
5. Continuing Education courses cannot be taken at your workplace.   _____

   _____
6. The only way to progress professionally is to take a full-time graduate course.   _____

   _____

c How do you feel about continuing education? Make notes on your opinions. Then discuss the advantages and disadvantages of each type of course with a partner. Use the phrases below wherever possible.

"cold" learning environment	limited socializing environment
study during free time	study at own speed
technical problems	expensive
study at your workplace	good opportunity to meet people

	Advantages	Disadvantages
1. Distance courses		
2. Full-time graduate course		
3. Conferences		
4. Refresher courses		
5. Part-time graduate courses		

d Read the list of continuing education courses. Check ✓ the ones you think would be suitable for each profession. Compare and justify your answers with your partner.

	Doctor	Lawyer	Structural Engineer	Your profession
Managing the Environment				
Improving your Interpersonal Skills				
Psychology of Violence in the Family				
Triumphant Managers				
Strategic Marketing				
Dietary Approaches to Prevention				
Taking Charge of Change				
Managing Technical People				
Employee's Rights				
Work-related Health and Safety				

credit *n*	a unit of a course at a school, university or college
lecture *n*	a speech on a topic usually at a university
deliver *n*	to give, to pass on
tutorial *n*	classes given to individual students
up-to-date *adj*	modern, state-of-the-art

Lesson 5
Internet changes distance education

a Survey your classmates and write their names in the right-hand column.

Find someone who . . .	Names
1. has a job.	
2. has taken some form of continuing education.	
3. wants to take an M.A. course abroad.	
4. would prefer a distance course to a full-time course.	
5. has registered for an online course.	

b Use the subheadings in the box to fill in the blanks on the online registration form below.

Designed for	Grading criteria	Venue	Course description	Fee

M.A.RKETING MANAGEMENT COURSE

Course Requirements: University transcripts, computer skills, proof of English competency (TOEFL / IELTS)

Outcome:	Certificate
(1)_____ :	Country University
Course category:	Online
Dates:	March 06 - June 06
(2)_____ :	US$1,700.00
Instructors:	Sherry Goodwin, PhD. and Kate Sumi, M.A.
(3)_____ :	Marketing undergraduates, graduates and employees
(4)_____ :	4 essays (25% each)
(5)_____ :	3-month online course that provides theory and practice in managing marketing
Course topics:	1st month: Creative strategies
	2nd month: Rethinking the process
	3rd month: Landing ideas

c Look at the types of information listed below. Check ✓ the information that is included in the electronic brochure above. Then design an electronic brochure for a course of your choosing which includes all the information below.

___ 1. number of hours

___ 2. course cost

___ 3. ending date

___ 4. document candidate will receive

___ 5. exam date

___ 6. passing grade

___ 7. course subjects

___ 8. location of the course

___ 9. essay deadlines

___ 10. course type

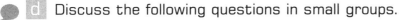

d Discuss the following questions in small groups.

1. Why is professional development important?

2. How frequently should a professional be updated?

3. What are the benefits of online courses?

e Listen to the recorded message. Number the lines in the order you hear them. Then fill in the blanks.

CD
T-2

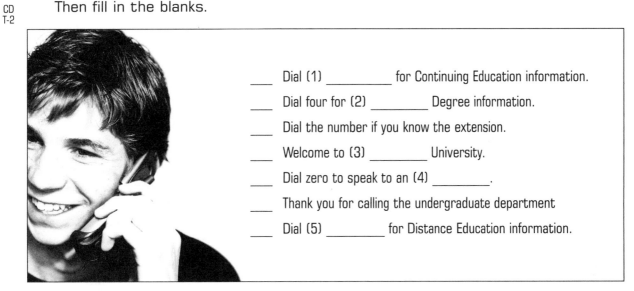

___ Dial (1) _____ for Continuing Education information.

___ Dial four for (2) _____ Degree information.

___ Dial the number if you know the extension.

___ Welcome to (3) _____ University.

___ Dial zero to speak to an (4) _____.

___ Thank you for calling the undergraduate department

___ Dial (5) _____ for Distance Education information.

f Which of the following are necessary if you are going to do an online distance course? Check the skills and compare your answers with those of a partner.

___ good reading skills

___ good interpersonal skills

___ computer skills

___ good oral presentation skills

___ perseverance

___ lots of free time

___ self-discipline

___ ability to listen to others

___ ability to work alone

___ extrovert personality

g Complete these contrary-to-fact sentences.

1. If Diego had more money, _____*he would register for a full time M.A. course.*_____

2. If he had the time, _____

3. If he were in the U.S., _____

4. He would have to improve his computer skills if _____

5. He would not miss Paula if _____

6. He would improve his chances of promotion if _____

Lesson 6

Being evaluated is rough

a Carla has just had her first performance review. Read what she says about it and then discuss the questions in groups.

I've just had my first three-month performance review with by my university professor. It was a rough experience. She pointed out things that I had never thought of. I was really nervous, but it was worth it!

- Have you ever had a review of your performance at college or work?
- If you have, how did you feel? Why?
- If you haven't, how do you think you would feel?
- What is the purpose of doing regular reviews?
- Do you prefer self-evaluation or someone giving you feedback? Why?

b Brainstorm a list of topics covered in a review. Compare your list with those of other groups.

Topics for performance evaluation:

_____ _____ _____

_____ _____ _____

_____ _____ _____

c Listen to Paula's first review with her M.A. advisor and fill in the missing words (1-5) on her review form. Then read her action plans and complete her goal statements.

CD T-3

Review Form

Strong points: Coping with the new (1) _____ , works hard, gets (2) _____ in on time

Weak points: Finds it (3) _____ to make new friends, problem with assignments, doesn't organize ideas in a (4) _____ manner

Not aware of: Not taking part in class discussions, needs to spend more time (5) _____

Goal 1: Going to try to participate more in (6) _____
    Action Plan: Will read up on the topics before the class

Goal 2: Going to get my assignments more (7) _____
    Action Plan: Read other students' essays

Goal 3: Find more time for (8) _____
    Action Plan: Change to evening shift

---

d Read the performance evaluation and complete with goals and action plans for Brian.

Performance Evaluation

Employee's name: *Brian Chen*
Reviewed by: *Steve Parker*
Strengths: *Takes feedback well; keen to grow professionally; is very responsible*
Weaknesses: *Time management; lack of experience*
Not aware of need to: *Organize priorities; communicate constantly with his manager*
Goal 1: *Improve time management skills*

    Action Plan: _____

_____

Goal 2: _____

    Action Plan: _____

_____

Goal 3: _____

    Action Plan: _____

_____

Date: _April 28_   **Time:** _12:00 p.m._

---

e Whose situation do the following statements refer to, Paula's or Brian's? Fill in the blanks with *P* (Paula) or *B* (Brian).

_____ 1. If I changed my shift, I would be able to do more reading.

_____ 2. If I were careful with time management, I'd meet deadlines without a doubt.

_____ 3. I would get better grades if I organized my work more logically.

_____ 4. I would be happier if I had some friends here.

_____ 5. If I communicated more frequently with my manager, I'd prioritize better.

f Imagine you are a teacher or work supervisor. Do a performance evaluation of a classmate and fill in the form below.

Name: _____

Reviewer: _____

Strong points: _____

_____

_____

Weak points: _____

_____

_____

Team Project 1

1 Work in groups of four. As a group, discuss the pros and cons of getting a job immediately after graduation or going on to some form of continuing education.

Getting a job

Pros	Cons
_____	_____
_____	_____
_____	_____
_____	_____

Continuing education

Pros	Cons
_____	_____
_____	_____
_____	_____
_____	_____

2 Discuss what would be the benefits of doing both, working and continuing with your education. Brainstorm a list of types of jobs that would allow you enough time to continue studying.

Types of jobs

_____	_____	_____
_____	_____	_____
_____	_____	_____

3 What kind of information would you need to make a decision about continuing your education? Decide on and check ✓ the five most important aspects you would need to research in order to make a decision.

____ university	____ course description	____ requirements
____ location	____ course length	____ scholarship / financial support
____ cost	____ accommodation	____ online courses
____ weather	____ degree / diploma	____ international student body

4 As a group, brainstorm ways that could help you do Internet research on the aspects you chose. Individually, research these aspects for your personal situation.

> *I went on collegeboard.com. It has great information . . .*

5 Compare answers. Discuss which university seems to be the best for you. Why? Share your research with the class.

Unit 2

Getting the job

I'd like to work here because . . .

a What qualities do companies look for in people when hiring personnel? Look at the following list and check ✓ the five most important qualities for each job.

	Secretary	Delivery Driver	Import / Export Manager	Attorney
experience				
good communication skills				
good references				
honesty and integrity				
lots of confidence				
problem-solving skills				
qualifications				
professional appearance				
strong leadership skills				

b In groups, compare your answers using sentences similar to those in the chart. Ask for and give your reasons.

If I were	hiring looking for employing taking on	a secretary,	professional appearance	would be wouldn't be	important. my top priority. crucial.

c Report your group's opinions to the class. Use the following sentences as models.

*When hiring a secretary, Aleksandra thinks qualifications are important, **but** Ian doesn't.*
***Both** Suzanna **and** Liz think that confidence is important when hiring a secretary.*
***Neither** Peter **nor** Jill thinks that leadership skills are important when employing a driver.*

d ARNORM Construction has openings for a variety of positions. The hiring manager has called a meeting of the Human Resources Department to discuss the qualifications he is looking for. Before you listen, look at the three vacant positions and tell your partner which you think are important qualities for each.

CD T-4

	Architect	Construction worker	Administrator
confidence			
dedication			
energy			
experience			
good communication skills			
honesty and integrity			
leadership skills			
perseverance			
problem solving skills			
professional appearance			
teamwork skills			

e With your partner select two ads from the same field. List the advantages and disadvantages of each position.

*I'd like to work here **because** the company has more benefits.*

OR

***Because** the company has more benefits, I'd like to work here.*

ABBREVIATIONS

exp'd = experienced
req'd = required
EOE = Equal Opportunity Employer
PhD = Doctor of Philosophy
PsyD = Doctor of Psychology

5 yrs = 5 years
immed. = immediately
w/ = with
bnfts = benefits
R&D = Research and Development

ENVIRONMENTAL ENGINEER — Petroleum refinery seeks individual w/5 yrs work experience in the field and a B.S. in Chemical or Industrial Engineering. Position requires strong communication, time management, and interpersonal skills. Benefits package and opportunity for advancement. Responsibilities will include R&D and field personnel supervision. Salary $72K. ANPETROL (907) 265-8000

ACCOUNTING OFFICE MANAGER — Art design company seeks individual w/minimum 5 years of accounting & managerial experience. Willing to train and motivate staff. Excellent interpersonal skills required. We offer: medical, dental, 401(k), profit sharing, vacation, sick and other great benefits. Salary $38,000. ektorasdesign@yahoo.com

ATTORNEY — San Francisco based company seeks exp'd contract attorney. Software licensing experience a plus. Excellent negotiation skills and ability to effectively find solutions under pressure req'd. California bar certification req'd. Occasional travel. Attractive compensation and benefits package offered. Salary based on experience. zicuzz@mailser.com.id EOE

ENGINEERING — HERFRI Construction company based in Germany needs skilled mechanical, and electrical engineers. Candidates must possess the ability to resolve complex technical problems and provide training as needed. Strong interpersonal skills required. Benefits include: profit sharing, medical, paid vacation, and leave. Starting salary $68K. Call 0049 572 909 95781, Fax 0049 306 909 95781

ACCOUNTING CLERK — Busy, fast-paced office has immed. opening for dependable person exp'd in Payroll & Accounts Receivables. Computer literate. Competitive compensation with medical/dental, 401(k) bnfts. $32K-$39K   EOE   redkloverbeer@contact.com

ATTORNEY — ExpressHRServices is currently looking for an exp'd attorney in labor relations and employment law. Bar admission in any state required. Must have knowledge of state and federal labor laws. Excellent written and verbal communication skills required. Frequent travel. Attractive salary and benefits. expresshrservices@nsm.ca   EOE

f In your notebook, create a classified ad. Include salary, job responsibilities and any other useful information.

Lesson 2

Dear Hiring Manager,

a When you are applying for a job, you usually send in a resume with a cover letter. Read the following sentences and write *A* (Agree) or *D* (Disagree).

1. A cover letter introduces you and your resume to an employer. _____

2. A cover letter is as important as a resume. _____

3. Cover letters demonstrate your writing skills. _____

4. One cover letter can be used for all employers. _____

5. A cover letter gives factual information and details about your career so far. _____

b Label the cover letter using the terms in the box. Five terms will not be used.

your address	savings account	formal closing	date
reason for writing	company's address	name	request to meet with the employer
signature	marital status	formal greeting	name of contact person
reason you are qualified			

A.J. Brown
21664 La Calera
San Juan Capistrano, CA 92707

Human Resources Department
ANPETROL
Glacier Road
Anchorage, AK 99800

Dear Hiring Manager,

Having several years of experience in the automotive, medical and insurance fields, I was excited to read about the opening for the position of sales manager as advertised on your Web site.

As you will see from my enclosed resume, I have taken various courses in communication skills, leadership, as well as quality control. Furthermore, my work experience has taught me to become customer-oriented, thus providing that all-important link between customer and company. To sum up, my extensive background would make me a valuable asset to your company.

I look forward to meeting you in person to discuss my skills. I can be reached at (714) 551-2972 or by e-mail at ajbrown@mymail.com. I hope that you will give the enclosed resume careful consideration.

Yours sincerely,

A.J. Brown

1. *your address*

2.

3.

4.

5.

6.

7.

8.

c Rewrite the following cover letter, using the correct punctuation and capitalization. Use the previous letter to help you.

> **marco martin**
> *justo sierra #2439*
> *col. ladrón de guevara*
> *guadalajara jalisco mexico 44600*
>
> **director of human resources**
> *green shield paint*
> *76 park road*
> *toronto, ontario 00378*
>
> dear hiring manager
>
> as an experienced professional in the industrial engineering field i am applying for the position of senior engineer as posted on your web site my excellent presentation skills and planning capabilities would be an asset to your company as you will notice in the enclosed resume i have the qualifications to make a valuable contribution to a top notch company like green shield paint my education and experience will show that i am the right candidate for the position furthermore i am currently pursuing a masters degree in business to better compete in this ever changing market i hope that i can have the opportunity to discuss my qualifications in a personal interview you can reach me at 7145512972 during regular business hours or send me an email at martin_marco@mymail.com.mx   sincerely marco martin

_____
_____
_____
_____
_____
_____
_____
_____
_____
_____
_____
_____
_____
_____
_____

d Write five sentences using the present perfect, describing the skills you have. Then read your sentences to a classmate.

1. *I have managed a team of 25 people.* _____
2. _____
3. _____
4. _____
5. _____

e In your notebook, write a cover letter for your resume. Use the cover letters in this lesson as models.

Lesson 3

This resume is impressive

a Which of these items would you include in a resume?

- ☐ previous salary
- ☐ reason for leaving last job
- ☐ expected salary
- ☐ reference
- ☐ social security number
- ☐ skills and qualifications

b You are going to hear a hiring manager and a colleague discussing a resume. Listen to the first part of their conversation and answer the questions.

CD T-5

1. What's the vacant post?
2. Why is the post vacant?

c Listen to the rest of the conversation and fill in the missing information on the resume.

CD T-6

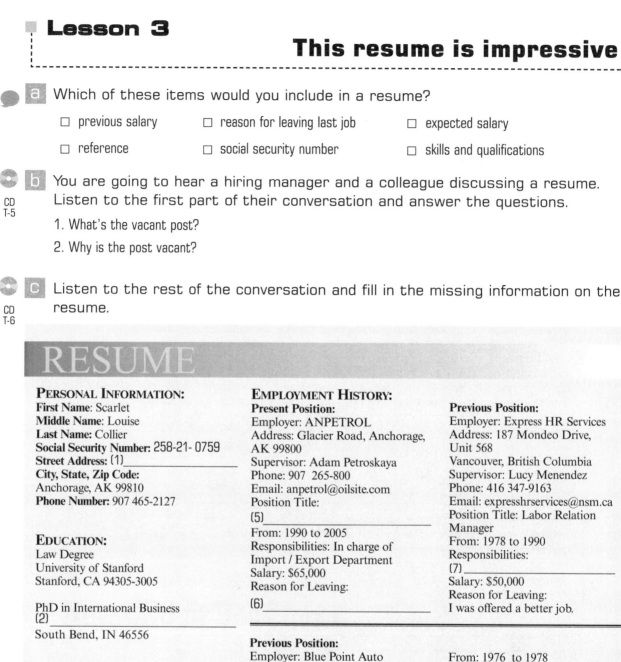

RESUME

PERSONAL INFORMATION:
First Name: Scarlet
Middle Name: Louise
Last Name: Collier
Social Security Number: 258-21- 0759
Street Address: (1)_____
City, State, Zip Code:
Anchorage, AK 99810
Phone Number: 907 465-2127

EDUCATION:
Law Degree
University of Stanford
Stanford, CA 94305-3005

PhD in International Business
(2)_____
South Bend, IN 46556

SKILLS AND QUALIFICATIONS:
Licenses, Skills Training Awards
Bar-certified in California and
Washington state
(3) _____
(4) _____

EMPLOYMENT HISTORY:
Present Position:
Employer: ANPETROL
Address: Glacier Road, Anchorage,
AK 99800
Supervisor: Adam Petroskaya
Phone: 907 265-800
Email: anpetrol@oilsite.com
Position Title:
(5)_____
From: 1990 to 2005
Responsibilities: In charge of
Import / Export Department
Salary: $65,000
Reason for Leaving:
(6)_____

Previous Position:
Employer: Blue Point Auto
Address: 4309 Main Street
Vancouver, British Columbia
Supervisor:
(8) _____
Phone: 416 414- 5688
Email: bluepoint@contact.com
Position Title: Import / Export
Assistant

Previous Position:
Employer: Express HR Services
Address: 187 Mondeo Drive,
Unit 568
Vancouver, British Columbia
Supervisor: Lucy Menendez
Phone: 416 347-9163
Email: expresshrservices@nsm.ca
Position Title: Labor Relation
Manager
From: 1978 to 1990
Responsibilities:
(7)_____
Salary: $50,000
Reason for Leaving:
I was offered a better job.

From: 1976 to 1978
Responsibilities: Assist the Labor
Manager
Salary: $32,000

References:
Furnished upon request

d With a partner look at the resume again and role-play Gunther and Tim's conversation.

Gunther: Hi, Tom. How's everything going?
Tim: Not too bad. Just looking over some job applications.
Gunther: Oh, yeah? What department?
Tim: The ...

e Study the following Grammar Review box and then complete the sentences with personal information.

Grammar Review		
Gerunds	**Infinitive**	**Gerund or Infinitive**
• The gerund is used after the following verbs: *enjoy, finish, give up, dislike* • The gerund is used after prepositions.	The infinitive is used after the following verbs: *want, plan, decide, would like*	The gerund or the infinitive can be used after the following verbs: *love, hate, like*
Examples Tim **enjoys interviewing** people. Scarlet is good **at giving** presentations.	**Examples** Gunther has **decided to have** his eyes checked. Tim **wants to call** Red Klover Beer.	**Examples** Amy **loves meeting** people. OR Amy **loves to meet** people.

1. I want *to get a good job with plenty of opportunity for promotion.*
2. I enjoy _____
3. I have decided _____
4. I'm good at _____
5. I plan _____
6. I dislike _____
7. I would like _____
8. I'm interested in _____
9. I hate _____
10. I have finished _____

f Survey your class and fill in the chart.

Do you like reading the business section of the newspaper? Why?

Find someone who . . .	Name	Reason
1. likes reading the business section of the newspaper.	*David*	*He is looking for a new job.*
2. hates talking in front of people.		
3. would like to get a scholarship.		
4. plans to take the TOEFL exam.		
5. wants to work abroad.		
6. enjoys working alone.		
7. wants to study for a Master's degree.		
8. likes doing interviews.		

Lesson 4

Writing your resume

A successful resume should tell not only what you have done in the past, but what you believe you could do in the future. Never feel you have nothing to write about. Take the time to think about yourself and plan carefully how you should write these things down to convince your future employer that you are the ideal candidate for the job he or she has to offer.

a To prepare for writing your resume, describe yourself to your partner as you focus on the following areas.

- experience
- interests
- skills
- personal qualities

b Make notes about who you are on the form below.

Experience
Include anything that refers to your education, any professional training, periods of employment, including part-time jobs or internships, any volunteer work, and any long periods of time in which you focused on a particular activity (e.g., foreign travel, language learning).

_____
_____
_____
_____

Interests
How you spend your spare time says a lot about your personality. Include other non-job-related skills you might have as a result of a personal interest or hobby.

_____
_____
_____
_____

Skills
Write down all your skills. If you have had previous work experience, no matter how short, ask yourself these questions.
- Which skills did I use here that I already had?
- Which skills did I improve on or consolidate?
- What new skills did I learn?

Also think about any activity you may have been involved in while at school or university that would have developed any of the following skills:

organizing events	supervising	giving advice
interviewing	meeting the public	making presentations
chairing meetings	training staff	trouble-shooting

_____
_____
_____
_____

Personal qualities
Write down any of the words from the box (on the opposite page) that you think apply to you. Use any other words that describe you as well.

_____
_____
_____
_____

accurate	careful	cooperative
adaptable	committed	courteous
creative	good time manager	practical
decisive	hardworking	relaxed
dedicated	independent worker	reliable
energetic	logical	self-confident
extrovert	loyal	self-motivated
flexible	methodical	thorough
friendly	orderly	works well under pressure
good communicator	organized	works well with others
good sense of humor	positive	

c There are two ways to write a resume: (1) by presenting your education and work experience chronologically (see the resume on page 20), or (2) by presenting your skills and qualities functionally. Read the functional resume below. Work with your partner to compare it to the one on page 20. Then answer the questions.

1. What does each resume tell you about the person who wrote it?

2. Which resume style is the most appropriate for you? Why?

Rachel Carter
145 Commercial Street
Boston, MA
Tel / fax: 617 367 5222

Profile
Self-confident, reliable graduate with a Postgraduate Art Restoration Diploma and excellent organizational skills. Able to work independently or with a team to a strict deadline. Has up-to-date computer skills and ample knowledge of digital photography and archiving.

Training
Has recently finished an Art Restoration Diploma at State University, Massachusetts

Skills gained
▶ Design
▶ Digital archiving
▶ Graphic reproduction
▶ Screen printing
▶ Technology of color reproduction
▶ Infrared photography

Experience
▶ Three months' work experience at the New England Textile Museum, with direct responsibility for archiving digital reproductions of the 18th & 19th century collections
▶ Restoration of water-damaged 18th century textiles

Education
B.A. Degree   Art History, *cum laude,* State University, Massachusetts
Diplomas   Art Restoration, National Museum Textile Design, New England Textile School

Interests
Reading science fiction
Photography
Watching movies

References
Dr. John Lowenstein, PhD   Mrs. Louise Carey
Department of Fine Arts   437 Pine St.
State University, MA   Salem, MA 01970

---

d Turn the notes you produced in exercise **b** into your resume. Use one of the two resumes as a model.

Lesson 5
If I were you, I would wear . . .

a Look at the following *DOs* and *DON'Ts*. Work with a partner and check the box if it applies to your country. Add any other advice that applies to your country.

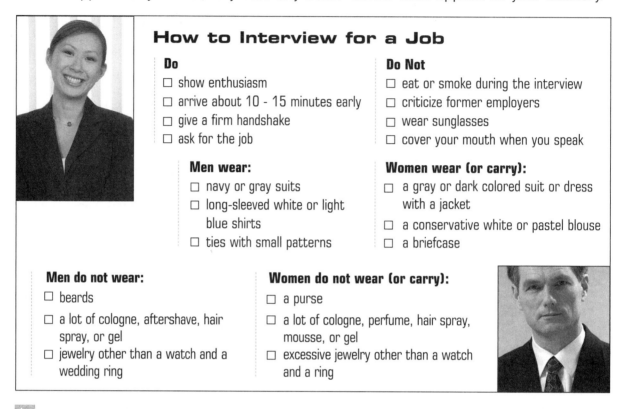

How to Interview for a Job

Do
- ☐ show enthusiasm
- ☐ arrive about 10 - 15 minutes early
- ☐ give a firm handshake
- ☐ ask for the job

Do Not
- ☐ eat or smoke during the interview
- ☐ criticize former employers
- ☐ wear sunglasses
- ☐ cover your mouth when you speak

Men wear:
- ☐ navy or gray suits
- ☐ long-sleeved white or light blue shirts
- ☐ ties with small patterns

Women wear (or carry):
- ☐ a gray or dark colored suit or dress with a jacket
- ☐ a conservative white or pastel blouse
- ☐ a briefcase

Men do not wear:
- ☐ beards
- ☐ a lot of cologne, aftershave, hair spray, or gel
- ☐ jewelry other than a watch and a wedding ring

Women do not wear (or carry):
- ☐ a purse
- ☐ a lot of cologne, perfume, hair spray, mousse, or gel
- ☐ excessive jewelry other than a watch and a ring

b Use the *DOs* and *DON'Ts* above to write advice to a friend who is going for an interview. Use expressions such as:

I think you should . . .	*If I were you, I would . . .*	*I don't think it's a good idea to . . .*
Wouldn't it be better to . . .	*Can I suggest that you . . .*	*Maybe you should . . .*

1. Your friend Tom is wearing a sports jacket and trousers with a check shirt.

_____

2. Your friend Sally is wearing a black suit, high heels, a red blouse, and sunglasses.

_____

3. Your friend asks you if you should kiss the hiring manager on the cheek.

_____

c Read the following sentences. Based on what you have read in the article and your own opinion, write *appropriate* OR *inappropriate*. Compare your answers with those of your partner.

The applicant . . .

1. thanked the hiring manager for the opportunity of meeting with him / her. _____
2. brought a dog to the interview and asked the receptionist to keep an eye on it. _____
3. chewed bubble gum during the interview. _____
4. laughed constantly throughout the interview. _____
5. came to the interview wearing a dark suit and black tie. _____

d Read the interviews and then work with a partner to answer the questions.

Interview 1

Robert: Good morning, Sylvia. How was your trip?

Sylvia: Fine thanks! For once the plane was on time!

Robert: Great! Now, I've read your resume and your cover letter. And I would like to ask you a few questions. First, can you tell me why you would like to join our company?

Sylvia: Sure. As you know, I've worked for a while in Import / Export and I've thoroughly enjoyed it.

Robert: Yes, that was with Blue Market in 2003. Can I ask you why you left the job?

Sylvia: Yes, I didn't find the job very challenging and I wanted something more demanding.

Robert: Oh, really? I spoke with your supervisor at Blue Market and she said that you were having problems with the new computers they were installing.

Sylvia: Well, yes. But I'm OK with computers now, at least most of the time.

Robert: OK. Let's move on then. For the last two years you have been working as a legal clerk and dealing with labor relations. How do you think that this experience will help you as an Import / Export Manager?

Sylvia: . . .

1. If you were Sylvia, how would you answer Robert's last question?

_____

2. Does Sylvia answer all the questions truthfully? Explain.

_____

Interview 2

Robert: Good afternoon, Mr. Gomez. You don't mind if I call you George, do you?

George: Not at all.

Robert: OK, George, take a seat and let's begin. First, can you tell me why you would like to join our company?

George: Well, I have been reading up about your company and I am very impressed. Your stock has increased steadily over the years, you have very low staff turnover, and your salaries are well above the market average. That's the sort of company that I would want to work in.

Robert: Thank you very much. Now can you tell me why you think you are suited to the job of Import / Export Manager?

George: Well, as you can see from my CV, I have been in Import and Export for the last three years and I have a Master's degree in International Business. However, I think what sets me apart from the others is my motivation. I love my work and I'm happy to work evenings and weekends when necessary.

Robert: . . .

3. If you were Robert, what question would you ask George next?

_____

4. How did George answer the questions differently from Sylvia?

_____

5. Who do you think should get the job? Why?

_____

e Use the classified ad that you wrote in Lesson 1 exercise **f** and role-play an interview with a partner.

Lesson 6

Interviews make me nervous

a Pretend you are going to a job interview next week. What will you do to prepare for it? With your partner make a list of five things you can do before and during the interview to ensure your success.

b Read the article and circle any recommendations for a successful interview that are similar to your own.

Tips for job interview

Worldwide, the idea of having to go to an interview is enough to make most people get nervous. Clammy hands, a rapid heartbeat and a shaky voice are normal reactions. But remember, you have been asked to interview because the employer thinks you might be the right person for the job. So take a deep breath and follow these steps that can help make your interview more successful.

Research the company

Find out information about the company you have applied to. What products or services do they sell? Where are they located? What type of persons do they employ? Visit their Web site and see how they promote themselves and their products or services. Talk to people you might know who work there and ask about working hours, dress code and daily tasks required for the position. This will show you are well informed and also help you ask important questions at the end of the interview.

Interview Dos

First impressions are important. The interview might take thirty minutes, but the first five minutes are the ones that will cause the strongest impression. Research shows that dress, body language and tone of voice all play a part in making a good first impression.

Dressing for success is crucial. Wear a conservative suit if you are interviewing for an office position. Dress more casually, but professionally if you are interviewing for a position in a factory warehouse or a less formal work site. You should avoid wearing excessive jewelry, perfume or loud colors.

Body language is a non-verbal statement about yourself. Make sure that your handshake is firm. This shows self-confidence. Good posture also demonstrates self-confidence and interest. Good eye contact is essential, too. It can help you recognize the interviewer's reaction to what you are saying. However, try not to stare at the interviewer.

The style, tone and delivery of your voice are also important. Be polite and professional. Try not to talk too fast as this could give the impression that you are nervous. Speak clearly and avoid hesitating too much so that you demonstrate confidence. In addition, try to relax and smile.

Ask questions

Finally, in some countries it is expected that the interviewee ask questions as this shows his / her interest in the position. If this is the case in your country, prepare your questions in advance. This is where your research comes in. It is your chance to ask questions about the position, requirements, and the expectations for the person who will fill the position. If the opportunity to ask these questions is not clearly presented, ask politely for a chance to do so.

c Discuss the answers to these questions with your partner.

1. Are these steps to a successful interview valid and important in your country?

2. Have you ever been to a job interview? What was it like?

d Listen to Ms. Edwards' job interview. Number the words and phrases in the order that you hear them.

CD
T-7

___ carry out	___ experience	___ key responsibilities
___ increased sales	___ in charge	___ implemented change
___ more efficient	___ trained	___ modified processes

e Listen again and write the questions that you hear.

CD
T-8

1. _____

2. _____

f Brainstorm additional questions that you might be asked to answer during an interview.

1. _____

2. _____

3. _____

4. _____

5. _____

g Imagine that you are going on a job interview. Decide on the company and the position you have applied for. Use the questions you wrote in exercise **f** to role-play an interview.

Good afternoon.
Please come in and
have a seat.

Thank you.

Team Project 2

In a group of four students, work as two teams.

Task:

1 As a group decide on a position and a specific company that is interested in filling that position. Use the cues below or your own ideas.

Web designer	Purchasing assistant	Advertising designer	Sales representative	Landscaper
	Human Resources assistant	Translator	Meteorologist	

2 Research the job opportunities for this position on the Internet so you can learn about any aspects related to the job that you are not sure of or for which you need more information. Use the Web sites below or key words related to the job you are researching to find an appropriate site.

collegegrad.com   quintcareers.com   smartjobguides.com   jobsearchtech.about.com

Team A: You are a company interested in filling a position.	**Team B:** You are a professional looking for a job.
Decide on the following. Write your ideas down clearly and practice any questions in preparation for interviewing candidates.	Decide and make notes and/or briefly practice talking about the following in preparation for your interview.
Company dress code	Educational experience *
Work schedule for the position	Work experience *
Responsibilities that the position will have	Specific qualities you possess
Qualities you are looking for in an employee	Professional goals and/or special interests
Salary and benefits	Questions you will ask the interviewer about the position
Questions you will ask at the interview	What you will wear at the interview
	Use information you would like to be true.

3 One student from each team will role-play the interview. Reread your notes.

4 Your teammates will observe the interview and write down suggestions to improve it. Exchange roles: observers become interviewer and interviewee.

5 Role-play the best interview in your group for the class. Vote on the most professional interview.

Unit 3

Relocating for work

Life is less formal here

a Look at the pictures and discuss your answers
to these questions with your partner.

1. In what country or countries would you expect to find these different houses or apartments?
2. In which one would you like to live? Why?
3. Which do you think is the most expensive and the least expensive? Why?

b Cordula Müller has recently been hired as marketing director of Ektoras
Design in Manhattan, New York. Prior to this, she worked in the regional
office of the company in Munich, Germany. She is talking to her new Mexican
colleague Fernanda Diaz about the differences between life in Munich, Mexico
and New York.

CD
T-9

Before you listen, try to guess what they will say. Then listen and check your answers.

1. Life is freer and more open in . . .
   _____ New York   _____ Munich
2. Life is quieter in . . .
   _____ Mexico _____ New York
3. People are friendlier in . . .
   _____ New York   _____ Mexico
4. Renting is really expensive in . . .
   _____ Munich   _____ Mexico

c Role-play a similar conversation with your partner. Compare life in other
countries or cities. Describe aspects such as *food, housing, job opportunities*
and *professional development opportunities.*

d Imagine that you need to relocate for a new job. Brainstorm six problems you run into when searching for an apartment.

_____   _____

_____   _____

_____   _____

e Read the article on apartment hunting tips. Underline the tips that will help you find an apartment.

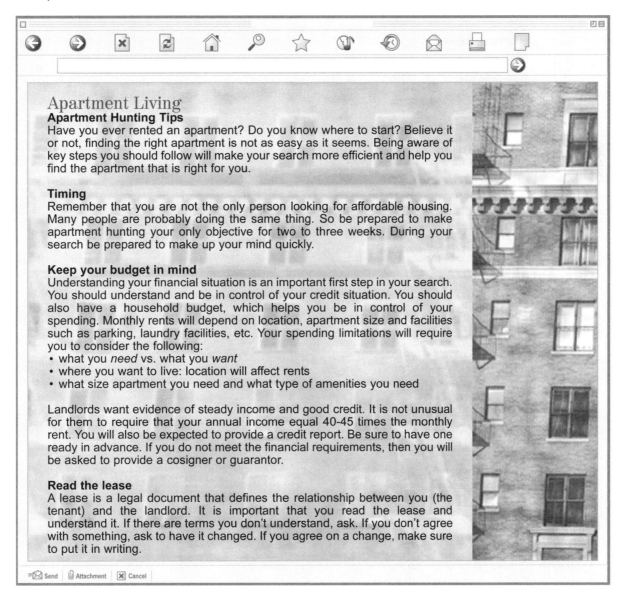

Apartment Living
Apartment Hunting Tips
Have you ever rented an apartment? Do you know where to start? Believe it or not, finding the right apartment is not as easy as it seems. Being aware of key steps you should follow will make your search more efficient and help you find the apartment that is right for you.

Timing
Remember that you are not the only person looking for affordable housing. Many people are probably doing the same thing. So be prepared to make apartment hunting your only objective for two to three weeks. During your search be prepared to make up your mind quickly.

Keep your budget in mind
Understanding your financial situation is an important first step in your search. You should understand and be in control of your credit situation. You should also have a household budget, which helps you be in control of your spending. Monthly rents will depend on location, apartment size and facilities such as parking, laundry facilities, etc. Your spending limitations will require you to consider the following:
• what you *need* vs. what you *want*
• where you want to live: location will affect rents
• what size apartment you need and what type of amenities you need

Landlords want evidence of steady income and good credit. It is not unusual for them to require that your annual income equal 40-45 times the monthly rent. You will also be expected to provide a credit report. Be sure to have one ready in advance. If you do not meet the financial requirements, then you will be asked to provide a cosigner or guarantor.

Read the lease
A lease is a legal document that defines the relationship between you (the tenant) and the landlord. It is important that you read the lease and understand it. If there are terms you don't understand, ask. If you don't agree with something, ask to have it changed. If you agree on a change, make sure to put it in writing.

Send | Attachment | Cancel

f Compare the list of problems you brainstormed in exercise **d**. Discuss with your partner how you could solve them. Refer to the article in exercise **e** for suggestions.

Lesson 2

We need to set goals

a What sort of person would you like as a roommate? Check ✓ the three you would most prefer. Then, in small groups, compare and discuss your answers.

☐ someone who likes the same type of music I do
☐ someone my own age
☐ a party animal
☐ someone who's fond of his / her family
☐ someone of the same sex
☐ someone of the opposite sex
☐ a good cook
☐ someone who is well-off
☐ a foreigner
☐ a part-time worker and student

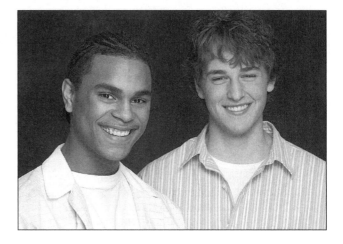

b Take the following test to find out the kind of roommate you would be.

ROOMMATES

I think that . . .	Yes	Maybe	No
1. An apartment is a place to rest and study. _____	☐	☐	☐
2. Unemployed people are not responsible. _____	☐	☐	☐
3. Jazz and classical music set me in the right mood to study. _____	☐	☐	☐
4. The kitchen must be immaculate all the time. _____	☐	☐	☐
5. Someone who has no sense of order and tidiness will never get anywhere in life. _____	☐	☐	☐
6. My belongings are sacred. I hate lending stuff to people. _____	☐	☐	☐
7. Coming back home after 10 p.m. is something I almost never do. ___	☐	☐	☐
8. Animals must stay away from people. Houses are for people. _____	☐	☐	☐
9. I prefer breathing clean air to smoky air. _____	☐	☐	☐
10. Emptying the fridge is a kind of theft. _____	☐	☐	☐

Score: 5 points for each **Yes**, 3 points for each **Maybe** and 1 point for each **No**.

What's your score?

10 - 23 points
It is hard for you to get along with roommates. You'd better live alone.

24 - 37 points
You are an average person. You can adapt somewhat easily to a roommate.

38 - 50 points
Even though you are responsible, you are a little bit too apprehensive. Chill out; life is neither black nor white. You could be a good roommate.

c Do you agree with the description of yourself? Explain to the class.

d Choose one of the writing activities below. Use your answers in exercises **a** and **b** to help you.

1. Write a short ad looking for a roommate to place on a university or company bulletin board.

> **Roommate wanted to share . . .**
>
> **Roommate will be entitled to . . .**
>
> **Roommate must . . .**

2. Write an e-mail to your best friend complaining about your new roommate. Give reasons for all the things you do not like about him or her.

> **Hey,**
> **I'm at the end of my rope. Today my roommate . . .**

3. Write a list of Dos and Don'ts for your new roommate.

> **Dos**
>
> **Don'ts**

4. Describe your ideal roommate.

e Find someone in the class who chose the same writing assignment as you did. Compare your papers. Report back to the class comparing your attitudes and giving reasons for your statements.

> *I was much less demanding with my roommate than Michael. I only asked that my roommate clean her room once a week. Michael wanted his roommate to make his bed every day.*

Lesson 3

There's so much to consider

 a Brainstorm a list of things that you would need to consider when looking for an apartment to rent. For example: *size, cost, location,* . . .

b Listen and check ✓ the important considerations for Cordula's family. Then check another five items that you think they would like.

CD
T-10

Terms and Conditions		Communal facilities	
Fee		Laundry facilities	
Deposit		Parking	
Late payment charges		Bike racks	
Length of lease*		**Safety**	
Utilities* included		Emergency exits	
Pets allowed		Fire extinguishers	
Physical Conditions		Gated entrance	
Heating		Intercom	
Air conditioning		Smoke detectors	
Number of bedrooms		**Kitchen**	
Cable TV / Internet connections		Counter space	
Natural light		Dishwasher	
Patio / balcony		Garbage disposal	
Storage			
View			
Location			
Noise level			
Public transportation proximity			
Distance from school / work			
Proximity of grocery, bank, etc.			

 c Compare your decisions about Cordula's family with those of a classmate. Give your reasons and reach an agreement. Use expressions such as:

Natural light is more important than bike racks because . . .

The most important consideration is pet rules because . . .

utility *n*	any basic necessity or service, e.g., water, electricity
lease *n*	a contract to pay to use a property

d Which of the following apartments would you choose for Cordula? Compare your answers with those of your partner.

1. Small cozy loft with high ceilings and brick wall - on ground floor - incredible deal $1000 per month - for music lovers only: band rehearsals in basement underneath 3 times a week at set hours.

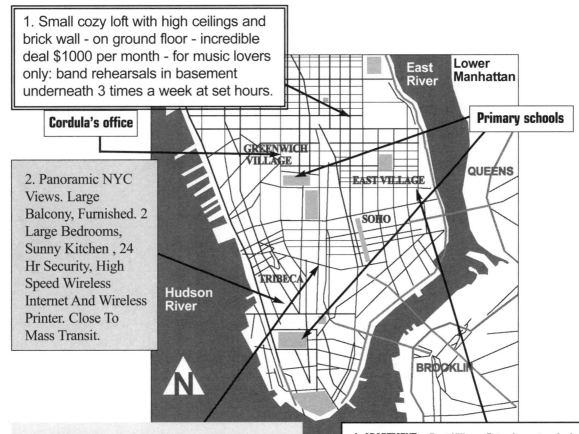

Cordula's office

East River

Lower Manhattan

Primary schools

GREENWICH VILLAGE

EAST VILLAGE

QUEENS

SOHO

TRIBECA

Hudson River

BROOKLIN

2. Panoramic NYC Views. Large Balcony, Furnished. 2 Large Bedrooms, Sunny Kitchen , 24 Hr Security, High Speed Wireless Internet And Wireless Printer. Close To Mass Transit.

3. EUROPE IN NEW YORK. Excellent place for a small family looking for a sunny, delightful apartment with a perfect location. Absolutely quiet and charming. Wood floors. Brand new air conditioning, new fridge, new microwave. Very modern design. Utilities not included. Please respond immediately. Absolutely no smoking.

4. APARTMENT: East Village. Extra large two bedroom apartment. Available furnished or unfurnished. New kitchen with top of the line appliances and cherry wood cabinets. Dark hardwood floors. Lots of closet space. Lots of natural light. Dining area.
BUILDING: Luxury 24 Hr full-service doorman building. Laundry on premises. Prime location.
RENT INCLUDES: Furniture, linens, kitchen equipment, TV and VCR. Maid service available at additional charge.

e Write a description of your perfect apartment.

My perfect apartment would . . .

Lesson 4

Dealing with the landlord

a When apartment hunting in your country, which of the following are important? Why? Compare your answers with those of your partner.

- ☐ Show up on time for your appointment with the landlord.
- ☐ Hire a broker or real estate agent.
- ☐ Have your personal credit report with you.
- ☐ Dress properly to see the landlord.
- ☐ Make a good impression on the landlord.
- ☐ Use the Internet to view the apartment beforehand.

b Listen to a real estate broker giving some tips on how to succeed in your apartment search. Then circle the letter that best completes the statement or answers the question.

CD
T-11

1. If a phone call is not returned by the next day, you should _____
   a. call again, one week later.
   b. not call again.
   c. call again; but with the utmost tact.

2. What's a frequent cause of losing good apartments?
   a. affordability
   b. indecision
   c. the lease conditions

3. What document is the broker advising you to fill out?
   a. an Apartments Unlimited application form
   b. a draft of the lease you'd like to sign
   c. a copy of the credit report

4. The broker advises _____
   a. dressing casually to impress the landlord.
   b. taking a shower before meeting the landlord.
   c. dressing and grooming professionally.

5. No-shows cause _____
   a. frustration for building managers.
   b. frustration for potential tenants.
   c. a great relief for building managers.

c Complete the dialogue using the sentences in the box.
Then practice it with a partner and improvise a continuation.

Will I need to make a deposit?

Do you mean you're separated,
divorced or something like that?

Would I be penalized for breaking the lease?

So, you're interested in the apartment?

What is your monthly income?

Landlord: (1) _____

Tenant: That's right, but first there are a few things I'd like to know about the apartment before I get to see it.

Landlord: I understand, but before I answer your questions let me get to know a little bit about you.
Do you have family?

Tenant: Yes, I do. I have a wife and daughter, but they are not living with me at the moment.

Landlord: Hmm . . . (2) _____

Tenant: No, no. Let me make myself clear. I come from Japan. I am relocating for a new job,
but my wife and daughter are still in Osaka. They will be coming once I settle in and prepare
a cozy home for them.

Landlord: Oh, I see. (3) _____

Tenant: The offer I got was for 70,000 dollars a year. By the way, how much is the rent?
(4) _____

Landlord: The rent is $1,200 a month and no, you wouldn't have to make a deposit.

Tenant: You have to understand that my wife's opinion will be crucial for taking the apartment.
(5) _____

Landlord: I'm afraid you would. But we can start with a three-month lease so that you can talk it over with your wife.

Tenant: Great. Now tell me about the apartment.

Landlord: Sure . . . what would you like to know?

d If you were looking for an apartment, what would you ask the landlord?
Write five questions.

1. _____
2. _____
3. _____
4. _____
5. _____

e Work with a partner to role-play a scene between a landlord and a future
tenant. Use the questions you both wrote for exercise **d** as a guide.

Lesson 5

Abbreviations drive me crazy

a Read these three dictionary definitions of a *loft*.
Which one fits the picture? Can you understand the ad?

Furnd loft,
nr d/town, EIK,
WIC, Immac Cond,
$1200 mo, Dep.
Req. 2345 3834 am

1. loft *n*	the space under the roof of a barn
2. loft *n*	an open area or part of one in a factory
3. loft *n*	a platform above a floor, such as a sleeping loft

b CD T-12 Listen to Cordula talking about her experience trying to find a loft and then answer the questions.

1. How is a loft different from an apartment?

_____

2. Why is Cordula looking for a loft?

_____

3. What are the four reasons Cordula gives for having difficulty finding a loft?
a. _____
b. _____
c. _____
d. _____

c Match the abbreviations with their meaning.

Abbreviations		Meaning		Abbreviations		Meaning
1. _____	off st pkng	a. condominium		11. _____	mo	k. immaculate condition
2. _____	EIK	b. walk-in closet		12. _____	W/D	l. fireplace
3. _____	dep req	c. off street parking		13. _____	ba	m. dishwasher
4. _____	Cond.	d. living room		14. _____	bdrm	n. bedroom
5. _____	priv	e. near		15. _____	F/P	o. hardwood floors
6. _____	nr	f. downtown		16. _____	immac cond	p. bathroom
7. _____	WIC	g. deposit required		17. _____	D/W	q. yard
8. _____	d/town	h. dining room		18. _____	hdwd flrs	r. washer and dryer
9. _____	liv	i. private		19. _____	yd	s. month
10. _____	din	j. eat in kitchen		20. _____	furnd	t. furnished

d Write out the following newspaper ads without abbreviations.

1.

> $650 mo, furnd, ac, w/d, HBO, phone, 507-625-5388 pm

1. *Furnished apartment with air conditioning.*
Includes washer and dryer, phone and cable TV.
$650 per month. Call 507-625-5388 in the evenings.

2.

> XTRA NICE 2 bdrm, hdwd flrs, closets, W/D, 3565-2277 after 3 pm

2. _____
_____
_____

3.

> 1 bdrm, furn kit, off st pkng, pool/Jacuzzi, MUST SEE! 857-1166

3. _____
_____
_____

4.

> 3647 AUBRY 2 bdrm, upstairs, WIC, F/P, EIK, dog friendly, priv yd $475/mo, no dep req

4. _____
_____
_____

5.

> 1 & 2 bdrm Montana Square, pool dep req No pets 274-96750

5. _____
_____
_____

6.

> 2 bdrm/1 ba, liv, kit, remodeled, hdwd flrs, $600/mo, 516-222-0446

6. _____
_____
_____

e With your partner, select one of the ads above. Role-play a telephone conversation between a landlord and a prospective tenant. The tenant should ask the landlord questions about the features mentioned in the ad. Once the landlord has answered the questions, the tenant should ask about items not mentioned in the ad, e.g., distance to shops, bank, etc. Select another ad and exchange roles.

Lesson 6

There are cockroaches everywhere

a Read the following clause of Cordula's lease agreement. Then read the statements below and check **T** for true, **F** for false or **?** for *It doesn't say*. Compare your answers and justify them.

Lessee shall:

(a) Keep all windows, window coverings, doors, locks and hardware in good, clean order and repair;

(b) Not hang any laundry (clothing, sheets, etc.) from any window, rail, porch or balcony, nor air or dry any of same within any yard area or space;

(c) Not cause or permit any locks or hooks to be placed upon any door or window without the prior written consent of Lessor;

(d) Maintain order at all times in the Premises and at all places on the Premises, and not make noise or otherwise disturb other residents;

(e) Keep all radios, television sets, stereos, phonographs, etc., turned down to a level of sound that does not annoy or interfere with other residents;

(f) Deposit all trash, garbage, rubbish or refuse in the locations provided therefore, and shall not allow any trash, garbage, rubbish or refuse to be deposited or permitted to stand on the exterior of any building or within the common elements;

	T	F	?
1. After doing their laundry residents can dry their clothes anywhere as long as it doesn't block the view inside the premises.			
2. New security devices can be installed if necessary.			
3. Residents have to get their neighbor's consent to play loud music.			
4. Tied trash bags can be deposited outside the apartment to be picked up.			
5. The lessor will be responsible for keeping all windows in good shape.			

b Before moving in Cordula wants to have some things fixed. Who would make the repairs? Match the problem with the right person.

a. an exterminator
b. a plumber
c. a handyman
d. a locksmith
e. an electrician

The kitchen sink is clogged. _____

The lock is jammed. _____

The faucet drips. _____

The heater doesn't work. _____

There are cockroaches everywhere. _____

The power is out. _____

C Listen to the three conversations and number the pictures below.
As you listen, identify the household problem each person has.
Write a sentence that describes the problem below each picture.

CD
T-13

Problem:

_____

_____

_____

_____

Problem:

_____

_____

_____

_____

Problem:

_____

_____

_____

_____

d Technicians and handymen make repairs for you when you don't have
the skills to fix these things yourself.
Form new sentences using the problems in exercise **b**.

1. *The heater doesn't work. I need to have (or get) the heater fixed.* _____

2. _____

3. _____

4. _____

5. _____

6. _____

e Look at the problems below. Decide which can be done by you and which need
to be done by somebody else. Compare your list with your partner's.

I can cut the grass myself, but I definitely need to get the roof fixed by a roofer.

	I'd do it myself	**I'd have it done**
An electric bulb is burned out.		
The grass is too tall.		
The roof leaks.		
The bathroom faucet drips.		

Team Project 3

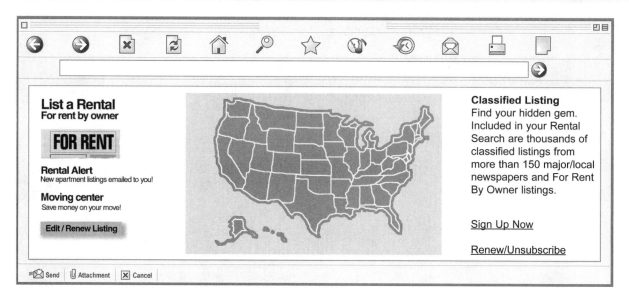

Task: Form a team with four or five students. You are going to write a rental ad
for a newspaper, bulletin board or Web site. Two members of the team will role-play an interview between the landlord of the property and potential tenants.
Invite tenants from other groups to speak to your landlord as members
of your team visit other landlords on other teams.

Role	Responsibility
Student 1 Team leader	Make sure everybody participates and speaks English.
Student 2 Secretary	Write up a draft of the ad based on the team members' ideas.
Student 3 Landlord	Prepare possible questions and answers that potential tenants might ask.
Student 4 Potential Tenant	Prepare possible questions and answers to use during the interview with the landlord.

Suggestions:

1. In your group discuss the features of the apartment you are going to include
   in the ad. You can use existing abbreviations or make up your own.
2. Once you come up with the final version of your ad post it on a desk
   or classroom wall where everyone on the team can see it.
3. The landlord will have to sit next to the ad to refer to it while speaking
   to the potential tenants.
4. Possible tenants should walk around the classroom and "phone" (sitting back
   to back) the landlords about the different apartments and make an appointment
   to see and talk about the apartment.
5. Landlords will have to choose the best candidates for tenant when they meet.

Follow-up: Use the internet to browse rental-related Web sites and find an apartment you'd like to rent. Role-play a
conversation following the suggested steps above.

Unit 4

Doing the job

a Ask two students the questions below and take notes on their answers.

	Student 1	Student 2
1. Do you sometimes have problems at school / work?		
2. What type of problems?		
3. What do you do to solve them? How do you decide what to do?		
4. Do you ask for advice when you have a problem? Why? Why not?		
5. Whom do you talk to about those problems? Why?		

b Below are the basic steps needed to solve any kind of problem. Match each one to the statement that exemplifies it. Then think of a problem you have at school / work and write four steps to solve it.

STEPS TO PROBLEM SOLVING

____ 1. Identify the problem.
____ 2. Find possible causes of the problem.
____ 3. Set goals* / objectives.
____ 4. Decide on an action plan to meet the goals / objectives.

EXAMPLES

a. I'm going to watch more English TV channels and try to find some American students to talk to.
b. In six months I want to be able to speak with a clear American accent.
c. I don't have enough contact with native speakers.
d. My English pronunciation is poor.

c Read the following newspaper article and answer the questions.

New CEO at Red Klover

F. Ward · correspondent

Red Klover Beer, Ireland's youngest beer company, has appointed a new Chief Executive Officer, Mr. Anatoly Kourchenko. Red Klover has seen a dramatic drop in profits over the last year prompting the resignation* of the former CEO.

Since its foundation 20 years ago, RKB has had a reputation for innovation. However, disaster struck last year when the company introduced a new product, Diet Draught. DD, as it was called, was launched with a massive advertising campaign*, but met with very poor market acceptance, and DD soon became known in the brewing* business as the *Disaster Drink*. The new product launch resulted in the substantial reduction of healthy company profits.

A company spokesperson, Mr. Damien Flynn, said that the directors were confident that Mr. Kourchenko would get to the root of the problem, set new goals and objectives, and oversee the design and implementation of action plans to resolve it.

1. Is Red Klover Beer an old and well-established company?
2. What does the abbreviation CEO stand for?
3. Why did the previous CEO resign?
4. Why did DD become known as the *Disaster Drink*?
5. What problem is Red Klover facing?
6. What will Mr. Kourchenko do to solve it?

d Look at the list of items that can cause problems for certain companies. Check ✓ the problems that these types of companies may face. Compare your answers with those of a partner and explain your choices.

	Car manufacturer	Internet server	Private hospital	Legal practice
raw material* (quality and cost)				
reliable, clean water supply				
inappropriate market study				
location				
production costs				
legal restrictions				
increase in fuel costs				
image				

e Mr. Kourchenko is addressing the board of directors. Check three topics that you think he will talk about. Then listen and confirm your predictions.

CD
T-14

- ☐ 1. the poor performance of the previous CEO
- ☐ 2. replacing staff
- ☐ 3. long-term* strategies for the company
- ☐ 4. his remuneration*
- ☐ 5. immediate plans

f Listen again and answer the questions.

CD
T-14

1. How would you describe Mr. Kourchenko's attitude?
_____

2. What percentage increase in domestic market share does he hope the company will achieve*?
_____

3. Where does he hope the company will export beer to?
_____

4. What will Mr. Kourchenko's first step be?
_____

5. Why do you think Mr. Kourchenko tells the directors that he will not hesitate in replacing staff who do not meet their goals in time? _____

achieve *v*	to reach, to gain
campaign *n*	an organized effort by people to reach a goal
brewing *n, adj*	making beer
goal *n*	an objective, a purpose
long-term *adj*	extending over a long period of time
remuneration *n*	payment for doing something, salary
resignation *n*	the act of choosing to leave one's post
raw material *n*	basic material needed to manufacture something

Lesson 2

a Listen to the meeting Mr. Kourchenko has with his managers and answer the questions.

CD T-15

1. How many people were at the meeting? _____

2. What are the two main causes of the reduced profit*? _____

3. Why does the company have more competitors*? _____

4. Where do the competitors come from? _____

5. What happened to the new type of beer they launched? _____

6. Why was the advertising budget* reduced? _____

b Listen to the meeting again and fill in the missing figures on the chart below.

CD T-15

Problem areas	Figures	
	Past	Present
1. High production costs	.75	.96
2. Annual Sales		
3. Competitors		
4. Advertising budget		
5. Profits		

c Look at the figures in the chart in exercise **b**. Describe the differences between the situations in the present and the situations in the past to your partner. Use the following sentence as a model.

Production costs used to be .75 and they have risen to .96.

budget *n*	an amount of money set aside for a specific purpose
competitor *n*	a product or company that competes with others for the same customers
measurable *adj*	capable of being measured
observable *adj*	capable of being observed
profit *n*	money remaining after business expenses are deducted
realistic *adj*	based on reality, not on something which is unlikely to happen

d Read the definiton of a *good goal*. Then grade the goals in the chart below by checking the correct column. Compare your answers with those of a partner.

A good goal _____

A goal is an objective. It is something that a person or a company wants to achieve in the future. Without a goal, we do not know where we are going. It gives us direction and a purpose. As Billy Sunday said, "More men fail through lack of purpose than lack of talent."

So, what is a good goal? A good business goal should be **realistic***, **observable*** and **measurable***. It should answer the question, *What do I want?*

GOALS	Realistic	Observable	Measurable
1. **Stove manufacturer:** We want to introduce a new model this year.	✓	✓	✓
2. **Multinational oil company:** We want to win the hearts and minds of the environmentalists.			
3. **Successful shoe company:** We want to enter the export market.			
4. **Small family hotel:** We want to compete with the Hilton Hotel.			
5. **Computer software company:** We want our staff to be happier.			
6. **Language school:** We want to start a kindergarten course.			

e Rewrite the poorly expressed goals from exercise **c** by adding the information they need.

1. _____
2. _____
3. _____
4. _____
5. _____

f Think of five goals for your personal, professional or academic life. Share them with your partner. Make sure they meet the standard of a good goal.
Then present two of your goals to the class.

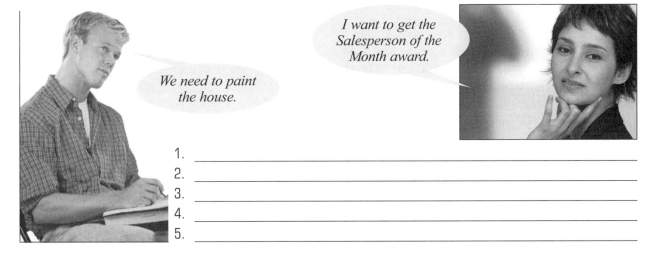

I want to get the Salesperson of the Month award.

We need to paint the house.

1. _____
2. _____
3. _____
4. _____
5. _____

Lesson 3

What's the action plan

a Read the text and then write an action plan for each goal.

> **An action plan** _____
>
> A goal tells you **what** you want to achieve, but it does not tell you **when** you are going to achieve it or **how** it is going to be achieved. This is the job of the **action plan**. In an action plan, you have to specify: 1) the *exact* result you want to get, i.e., a very specific goal, 2) in what time frame, and 3) what steps you are going to take to achieve the goal.

1. GOAL: My goal is to lose weight.
   ACTION PLAN: *I am going to lose 10 pounds in eight weeks, so I am going to go on a diet and exercise 15 minutes a day.*

2. GOAL: I want to learn English.
   ACTION PLAN: _____

3. GOAL: The company needs to increase sales.
   ACTION PLAN: _____

4. GOAL: I want to study / work in an English-speaking country.
   ACTION PLAN: _____

5. GOAL: The company needs to reduce production costs.
   ACTION PLAN: _____

b Read the action plans set by the managers at Red Klover Beer. Fill in the blanks with the appropriate goals from the options in the box. Compare your choices with those of your partner.

launch a new product		increase sales		export beer
	optimize* production		obtain certification	

1. Ms. Kimberly Edwards, Sales Manager
GOAL: _____
ACTION PLAN: Carry out a customer needs analysis and a distribution analysis in four weeks.
Then, establish sales objectives and plan the advertising campaign.

2. Mr. Kenji Shibuya, Senior Manager of the Engineering Department
GOAL: _____
ACTION PLAN: Analyze operation and production systems and implement* a strict maintenance* program within the production process before December. Implement a training* program in both time management* and optimal use of equipment and machinery for the entire production team by February.

3. Ms. Alexandra M. Parks, Quality Control Manager
GOAL: _____
ACTION PLAN: Modify and improve* all quality systems and procedures in the company within the year with the help of QS (Quality Systems) and QA (Quality Assurance) teams that will be in charge of developing procedures, and manuals and auditing all production areas.

c Discuss these questions in groups.

- Are the proposed plans in exercise **b** good action plans? Give your reasons.
- How could you improve the goals? Do you think these action plans can improve Red Klover Beer's situation?

d What does the following quotation mean? Think of an example to illustrate it. Discuss your opinions with your partner.

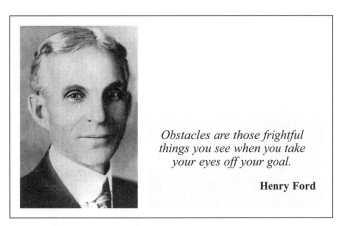

Obstacles are those frightful things you see when you take your eyes off your goal.

Henry Ford

e Match the obstacles below with their possible solutions.

Obstacles

___ 1. The analysis indicated that the strong competition from foreign beers is a serious obstacle, and it affects the goal of increasing sales in the short term.

___ 2. The optimization of production is not possible because some machines are old and need repair or replacement.

___ 3. With the current personnel available a year is not enough to develop the procedure* manuals for all company departments.

___ 4. Launching a new product that is more competitive in the market would require reducing investment in other action plans.

Solutions

a. The company should initiate a maintenance* program and also acquire new equipment.

b. The company should focus on improving the advertising of existing products and work on new product development at a later stage.

c. The new sales objectives have to be realistic and based on the company's current situation. The advertising campaign should have a short and a long-term objective.

d. Both the Quality Systems and the Quality Assurance departments need to increase their teams.

f Role-play this situation. You are in charge of one of the departments at Red Klover Beer and your partner is a colleague. Identify a goal and talk about the obstacles to achieving your goal. Discuss the possible solutions. Use phrases from the chart below.

Talking about obstacles	Talking about solutions
I have to . . . but . . .	*I think you can / could . . .*
There is a problem with . . . because . . .	*You should . . .*
I can't . . . because . . .	*I consider that . . .*
The . . . isn't working.	*Why don't you . . .*
The . . . are below target.	*You need to . . .*

implement *v*	to start, to put in to action	**management** *n*	the art and science of directing a business
improve *v*	to make something better	**optimize** *v*	to get the best outcome possible
maintenance *n*	keeping equipment, machinery in good working order	**procedure** *n*	detailed steps for doing something
		training *n*	a process of education, instruction

Lesson 4

It's time for a decision

a In small groups, discuss reasons a company can have for letting an employee go. Do you agree with these reasons?

CD
T-16

b Listen to Mr. Kourchenko discussing the marketing manager's future with his assistant Jane McCartney. Fill in the chart with the reasons FOR and AGAINST letting Mr. Webber go.

Mr. Kourchenko's reasons FOR letting Mr. Webber go.	Ms. McCartney's reasons AGAINST letting Mr. Webber go.
1.	1.
2.	2.
3.	3.

c Choose one of the following situations. Work in pairs and write the arguments FOR and AGAINST the particular situation. Then role-play the situation using the conversation in exercise **b** as a model.

1 The production department, under Mr. Shibuya, has implemented a maintenance program, and this has reduced production costs, but they are still higher than others in the industry. Mr. Kourchenko is considering downsizing* the production line workforce* to reduce costs further. Mr. Shibuya doesn't agree.

2 Ms. Parks has started the process of international certification for quality control, but it will take at least one year. Mr. Kourchenko thinks this is too long and would like to cancel the certification process.

d Read the following letter and add the missing relative pronouns.

17 March, _____

Dear Jim,

As you know, you are someone (1) _____ opinion is highly respected in this company, and the people (2) _____ have worked with you *will agree* that you have done some truly excellent work. Your loyalty* is something (3) _____ has been highly valued. The company has benefited greatly from the service (4) _____ you have given us over the years.

However, I regret to inform you that I have had to make the decision to release you from your obligations to the company. You are fully aware that Red Klover is a company (5) _____ respects its employees and (6) _____ has a reputation for fairness. I am therefore happy to inform you that we are offering you a retirement* package (7) _____ will allow you to take early retirement. If, however, you intend to look for further employment, I would be very happy to write you a reference (8) _____ will portray you as a highly reliable person (9) _____ would be an asset* to any company.

Yours sincerely,

Anatoly Kourchenko

| Anatoly Kourchenko
| CEO
| Red Klover Beers

e Look at the letter again. Circle the collocations from the chart below that are used in the letter.

adv / adj	respected	valued	aware	excellent	happy	reliable	appreciated	satisfied
highly	✓	✓	✓			✓	✓	✓
fully			✓					
greatly	✓	✓					✓	
truly	✓	✓		✓	✓		✓	✓
very			✓		✓	✓		✓

f Use the collocation chart as a guide to find and circle the errors in the following sentences.

1. You have done some very excellent work and we are greatly satisfied with your input.
2. We all agree that you are a fully reliable worker and your performance is greatly appreciated.
3. I am highly happy to award you the Salesperson of the Year for your truly excellent work.
4. The directors were fully satisfied with the CEO's report but were not highly happy with his budget.
5. I am greatly aware that her contributions in meetings are highly appreciated.

asset *n*	an advantage, a benefit
downsize *v*	to reduce the number of employees in a company
loyalty *n*	faithfulness, devotion, allegiance
retirement *n*	stopping work due to age or poor health
workforce *n*	all employed workers in a company

Lesson 5

We need time management training

The bad news is time flies.
The good news is you're the pilot. **Michael Altshuler**

a Discuss the following questions with your partner.

- Why is it important to organize your time?
- If you have a lot of important things to do, how do you decide what to do first?
- How do you organize your time?

b Here are four ways to prioritize your work. Rank them from 1 (most important) to 4 (least important). Justify your decisions to a classmate.

___ Identify the task you have to carry out.
___ Decide if the task or activity is important.
___ Set a deadline for the task.
___ Determine how long the task will take.

c Read Ms. Parks' job list. Complete her Weekly Planner so that she uses her time effectively.

Job list	Important	Urgent	Deadline	Time needed
Review procedure manuals	very	not very	by end of week	8 hrs.
Talk to suppliers	not very		by end of week	2 hrs.
Evaluate the Quality Systems and the Quality Assurance teams	essential	not very	by Tues. 5:00 p.m.	12 hrs.
Speak to the cleaner about washing windows	not very	no	none	20 mins.
Start internal audit	yes	not very	end of the month	15 hrs.
Interview candidates for position of assistant to my department	yes	extremely	by Thurs. at 2:00 p.m.	3 hrs.
Check e-mail and answer letters daily	yes	no	none	1 hr. every day

Weekly Planner

	Monday	Tuesday	Wednesday	Thursday	Friday
8:30 *Arrive at work*					
1:00 - 1:30 *Lunch*					
5:00 *Leave the office*					

d Mr. Kourchenko is having a discussion. Listen and answer the questions.

CD T-17

1. Who is Mr. Kourchenko talking to? _____

2. What is he talking about? _____

e Listen again and complete the timetable.

CD T-17

Task	Person in charge	Description of the process	Start date	End date	Expected result
1.	Ms. Edwards		October 3rd		a report
2. design a continuous training program		decide on number of training hours; organize sessions across two weeks		October 24th	

f Form a group to discuss the answers to these questions.

1. In what cases do you think a timetable like the one in exercise **e** is useful?
2. Is it just for a company?
3. How could it be useful for you?
4. Why?

g Study the expressions in the chart below. Then use them to complete the sentences.

Expression	Definition	Example
due	scheduled	The *due* date for the report is tomorrow.
on time	at the right time; not sooner, not later	I'm never late. I always arrive *on time*.
in time	to have something ready by the deadline	I need this by Wednesday. Will it be ready *in time*?
be running late	to be behind schedule, to be late	It's 10:30. The meeting should have finished at 10:00. They *'re running late* again.
ahead of time	early, before a certain time	Susan has already finished the project due next week. She's always *ahead of time*.
time consuming	requiring a lot of time	Searching the net for information is very *time-consuming*.

1. Researching all the facts can be very _____.
2. If you don't arrive _____ for the meeting, we'll have to start without you.
3. Sarah doesn't seem to be around. She must _____ again.
4. Do you think we'll get the machinery fixed _____ to meet next month's production targets?
5. The new office equipment is _____ to arrive by the end of the month.
6. You're _____; the deadline for this is in two weeks.

Lesson 6
Who's the new marketing manager

a Red Klover needs a new marketing manager. Rank the selection criteria from 1 (most important) to 9 (least important). Compare your answers with those of your partner. Justify your answers.

___ typing skills	___ physical appearance	___ age
___ fashion sense	___ experience	___ attitude / personality
___ professional profile* / skills	___ gender	___ punctuality

b Match the characteristics of a good marketing manager with the definitions.

Characteristics of a good marketing manager	Definitions
___ 1. creative	a. able to reach objectives without giving up, always searching for solutions
___ 2. knowledgeable*	b. knowing the market and the competitors, spotting opportunities, and putting all this information to use
___ 3. organized	c. knowing how to develop the company and / or product image*
___ 4. persistent*	d. dealing with* clients and suppliers successfully
___ 5. good interpersonal skills	e. able to arrange for things to happen when, where and how they are needed

c Write the criteria you would use for the following decisions. Compare your answers with those of your group.

1. Selecting a Master's program

_____ *Cost, Length of course, . . .* _____

2. Hiring a secretary

_____

_____

3. Choosing a job

_____

_____

accounting *n, adj*	the profession of a person who keeps records of a company's finances
deal with *v*	to interact with someone
image *n*	a company's or a person's appearance to others
knowledgeable *adj*	having information on or familiarity with something
persistent *adj*	persevering, never quitting
profile *n*	a group of characteristics

CD T-18 **d** Read the profiles of three candidates for the Marketing Manager position. Work with a partner and decide whom you would choose. Then listen to the conversation and confirm your prediction.

Candidate 1

A.J. Bundy: male, 30 years old, single

Education: undergraduate studies in Marketing, degree not awarded

Current position: salesman, 2 years experience, awarded Best Salesman of the Year

Personality: intelligent, excellent communicator, self-motivated, persistent: doesn't take *no* for an answer

Candidate 2

Sarah E. Mackenzie: female, 52 years old, married

Education: B.A. in Business Administration

Current position: Deputy Marketing Manager for 4-years, with previous experience as manager in a former job

Personality: demanding, sensitive, energetic, punctual

Candidate 3

Krista Higgins: female, 38 years old, single

Education: B.A. in Accounting*

Current position: Assistant Manager of Sales Department, 2-year seniority

Personality: organized, responsible, impatient, good people skills

e Listen again and decide if the following sentences are *true* or *false*. If *false*, correct the statement.

CD T-18

1. Mr. Kourchenko wants to hire someone from outside the company with more experience. _____

   _____

2. A.J. Bundy is the best candidate because he is very persistent. _____

   _____

3. Mr. Kourchenko thinks that the Deputy Marketing Manager is a very good option for the opening. _____

   _____

4. The final decision was made by Mr. Kourchenko. _____

   _____

f Answer the following questions in your notebook. Discuss your answers with your partner.

1. Why do you think Mr. Kourchenko is asking his committee for their opinion?
2. Why is it important for Mr. Kourchenko to promote someone from inside the company?
3. Why do you think it is important for the candidate to have good interpersonal skills?
4. Do you think marketing experience is essential? Why?
5. How do they make the decision about who will be promoted?

Team Project 4

Select one of the role cards below. Role-play the situation with your partner.
Prepare your goal chart and present it to the class.

Student A: You want to be an exchange student for one semester at a university in the United States. The university requires you to get a minimum of 550 points on the TOEFL (Test of English as a Foreign Language). You took the exam and got a 480. You have seven months to prepare for a second TOEFL exam. However you are currently working part-time, so you do not have much time to study.

Describe your situation to student B and ask him/her for advice. What are you going to do? How are you going to make the best use of your time?

Now make a goal chart and present it to the class.

Student B: You are a student working part-time and studying English. There will be an opening for a better position at your company in two months. All candidates must pass several exams; one of them is an English test. You only have two months to prepare for the position and improve your English.

Describe your situation to student A and ask him/her for advice. What are you going to do? How are you going to make the best use of your time?

Now make a goal chart and present it to the class.

Student A / Goal:		
Action plan(s)	Time (start and completion dates)	Specific result(s)

Student B / Goal:		
Action plan(s)	Time (start and completion dates)	Specific result(s)

Unit 5

Solving problems

Where's the shipment

a Work with a partner and discuss the following questions.

- What type of products do companies ship*?
- How is merchandise shipped?
- What sort of things can go wrong?

b Listen to the following conversation between two colleagues and answer the questions.

CD
T-19

1. When was ARNO Medical Center supposed to receive their order?

_____

2. What medications were ordered?

_____

3. Why hasn't their order arrived?

_____

4. When should ARNO Medical Center receive their order?

_____

5. What other products does Wayne want to know if they have in stock*?

_____
_____

c Role-play a conversation similar to the one in exercise **b**. Use the flow chart below as a guide.

```
Greet  ─────────────────────────────────→  Respond, then ask
                                            about an order
                                                  │
Answer, then  ←───────────────────────────────────┘
give information  ─────────────────────→  Ask for delivery date
                                                  │
Answer  ←─────────────────────────────────────────┘
        ─────────────────────────────→  Respond, ask about
                                        other items in stock
                                                  │
Don't know but  ←─────────────────────────────────┘
will check stock  ─────────────────────→  Respond
```

back order *n*	a delayed order due to item not being in stock
drum *n*	a barrel made from metal
iodine *n*	a brownish-orange chemical element used in medicine
merchandise *n*	items, goods made for sale at the retail level
ship *v*	to send something
stock *n*	items that are kept by a company for sale or use

d Rewrite the following statements and questions by embedding the direct question in parentheses.

1. I don't know . . . (Where is the invoice?) *I don't know where the invoice is.*

2. I forgot . . . (Where did you leave the order?)

   _____

3. Do you have any idea . . . (How do you classify the merchandise*?)

   _____

4. Can you tell me . . . (Why does he need extra packing material?)

   _____

5. I don't remember . . . (What time is our meeting?)

   _____

6. Do you know . . . (Who is the new shipping clerk?)

   _____

7. I have no idea . . . (What have they packed?)

   _____

8. I'm not sure . . . (What time is the truck arriving tomorrow?)

   _____

9. Do you know . . . (Why isn't the forklift working?)

   _____

e Complete the conversation. Choose the correct question from the box and embed it in the questions and statements below.

When can you start?		When will I have Internet access?
What is that area?	Where are you from?	What are they doing?

Mike: Have a seat, Mr. Li.

Chung: Thank you, sir. And please . . . call me Chung.

Mike: OK. But you have to call me Mike. So . . . why don't you tell me (1) ___*where you're from.*___

Chung: I'm originally from South Korea, but my family moved to the United States when I was very young.

Mike: Can I ask you (2) _____

Chung: Well, I can start today!.

Mike: Great. Would you like to have a look around the premises?

Chung: Sounds great.

Mike: Now, over there is accounting and next to it is the sales department.

Chung: Mike, do you know (3) _____

Mike: Sure. That section is going to be the new conference room.

Chung: Could you tell me (4) _____

Mike: Well, they're installing fiber optic cable . . . and those guys are working on the new phone system. OK. This is your desk.

Chung: Great. Can you tell me (5) _____

Mike: I think it will be ready tomorrow. Any other questions?

Chung: No, I think that's it.

Lesson 2

When do we get our stuff

a Spoken language is often informal. Academic and business communication is usually formal. Brainstorm a list of informal words and expressions and their formal equivalents. Share your list with the class.

Informal	Formal
How are things?	*How have you been?*

b Order the sentences below to make a telephone conversation. Then circle the informal phrases and expressions.

___1___ **Wayne:** Hi. Is that Shelley?

_____ **Wayne:** Yeah! Bad news. The disinfectant is out of stock.

_____ **Shelley:** Hi, Wayne. Any news on my order for the disinfectant and the NAMIL?

_____ **Shelley:** Hey, stop winding me up! So when do we get it?

_____ **Wayne:** But the good news is that it's due in tomorrow.

_____ **Shelley:** Out of stock! Oh, no. My boss will kill me.

_____ **Wayne:** Sure thing, Shelley. I'll get an e-mail off right away.

_____ **Shelley:** Well, Wayne. You're just one efficient guy. Hopefully the news will get my boss to stop breathing down my neck. Appreciate the call. Talk to you later.

_____ **Shelley:** OK. Thursday's cool. Look, do you think you could put that down in writing because my boss is blaming me.

_____ **Wayne:** I'll send it off right away. You should have it by Thursday.

c In your notebook write the letter Wayne would send to Shelley. Use the formal expressions below.

pleased to inform you that	regret any inconvenience*	dispatch*

Formal	Informal
take delivery of *v*	receive, get
dispatch *v*	send it, send it off, get it off
refund *v*	send money back
inconvenience *n*	trouble, hassle

d Match the informal expressions in the box with the formal expressions in the letter.

ARNO MEDICAL CENTER
577 Grand Avenue
Bangor, Maine 04401
(207)942-2468

AMC

Informal expressions
___ 1. We got the stuff.
___ 2. We want you to . . .
___ 3. by plane
___ 4. We're sending them back.
___ 5. We want our money back.
___ 6. Also, . . .
___ 7. You didn't send them.
___ 8. The boxes got wet.
___ 9. So, get to it.
___ 10. And you pick up the tab.

PHARMAQWIK
Attn: Wayne Hansen
2405 Cactus Drive
Phoenix, AZ 9906
June 17,

Sir or Madam:
On June 7 of this year we ordered (purchase order #A000031) and
(a) <u>subsequently took delivery* of the following merchandise</u>:

Quantity Ordered	Description	Lot Number
5000	NAPIL-30	2005-216
5000	NAPIL-50	2005-306
5000	NAPIL-80	2005-212
40 drums	disinfectant	

Your company packed our order in thirty-five (35) boxes. Unfortunately, twelve of the boxes were damaged during shipping. These (b) <u>boxes have suffered water damage,</u> which in turn has damaged the labels of the product. The products affected are NAPIL 80, lot #2005-212 and NAPIL 30, lot #306. (c) <u>We are therefore returning the damaged boxes</u> and would like (d) <u>to be refunded*</u> for shipping costs. (e) <u>In addition,</u> we ordered 40 drums of disinfectant that were listed on the packing list but (f) <u>they were not delivered</u>. We are still interested in receiving the disinfectant and the damaged merchandise; however, (g) <u>we ask that</u> you place the merchandise on purchase orders #A000101 and #A000102, respectively. We also ask that you ship purchase order #A000102 (h) <u>via air freight</u> (i) <u>at your expense</u>. (j) <u>I look forward to your reply and a resolution to our problem.</u>

Sincerely,
Shelley Roberts

e Choose one of the two options below and write a complaint letter of your own.

1. On February 16, you made dinner reservations for 7:30 at DJ's Bistro, a prestigious restaurant, to entertain a business client. After waiting patiently for 45 minutes, you ask the maitre d' to find out what the delay is and he rudely tells you to wait. Your guest is angry. Write a letter of complaint to DJ's Bistro explaining the problem.

2. You have just received the May statement from your charge account #05131999 at Marie Clementine Boutique. The total amount is $513.19. However, you notice that there is a charge for $312.58 for a suit purchased on May 13. You know that the transaction is an error because you did not buy that suit. You were also out of town that week and you have plane tickets and hotel receipts to prove you were not in town. Write a letter of complaint to Marie Clementine Boutique asking to be reimbursed.

Let's call a meeting

a Interview two students. Take notes on their answers.

	Student 1	Student 2
1. Do you enjoy meetings? Why / Why not?		
2. What do you think are the characteristics of a good meeting?		
3. What do you think are the characteristics of a bad meeting?		
4. What things do you have to think about when planning a meeting?		

b Listen to the conversation between Walter Keaton, president of ARNO, and his secretary, Nicole Mancuso. Fill in the missing information on the Agenda.

CD T-20

Weekly Meeting:

Agenda

Date and Time	03-May-06
Venue*	

Meeting called by:	Walter Keaton	Minutes*:	
Chairperson*:	Walter Keaton	Attendees:	
Timekeeper:	Nicole Mancuso		
Please read:			
Please bring:			

Topic	Time Limit	Objective	Action Points	Person	Deadline*
1. Replacing equipment	45 Mins.	To make a list of priorities of equipment that needs replacing			
2. Loss of market share	60 Mins.	To identify causes of market loss and develop a strategy and timeline for reversing situation			
3. Lawsuit	30 Mins.	To get information for defense case			

c Fill the blanks. Then work with a partner and answer the questions.

1. Why is it a good idea to circulate* the a _ _ _ _ _ a few days before the meeting?
   _____

2. Why is the v _ _ _ _ important?
   _____

3. Do you think the c _ _ _ _ _ _ _ _ _ _ _ should participate in the discussions or simply manage the meeting? Why?
   _____

4. Why is it necessary to take m _ _ _ _ _ _ in a meeting?
   _____

5. Why does each topic on the agenda* have a t_ _ _ _ _ _ _ _ _ ?
   _____

d Read the paragraph on setting meeting objectives. Complete the chart.

Setting Meeting Objectives

A meeting that has no written objectives, or poor objectives, will almost certainly be a failure. People need to know what they are hoping to achieve. Good objectives for a meeting should be specific, concrete and produce action points.

Poor objective	Reason	Improved objective
1. To inform staff that they need to improve efficiency.	Simply informing staff will not guarantee results	To identify ways to improve efficiency and set a time line for implementation.
2. To talk about downsizing the workforce.		
3. To write a report.		
4. To discuss the problem of poor sales.		

e Study the chart. Tell your partner whether you agree with the graph. Give reasons to justify your opinions.

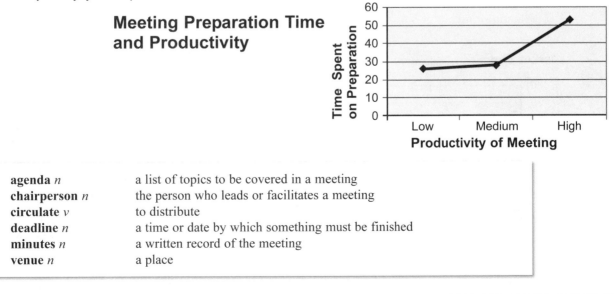

Meeting Preparation Time and Productivity

Time Spent on Preparation

Productivity of Meeting: Low, Medium, High

agenda *n*	a list of topics to be covered in a meeting
chairperson *n*	the person who leads or facilitates a meeting
circulate *v*	to distribute
deadline *n*	a time or date by which something must be finished
minutes *n*	a written record of the meeting
venue *n*	a place

Lesson 4

As you can see on the diagram . . .

a Discuss the questions below in groups. Keep notes of your ideas in your notebook.

- What is the purpose of using diagrams?
- What kind of information can be presented in a diagram?

b Label the diagrams.

| Pyramid | Hierarchical or Organizational | Cycle | Venn | Flow Chart | Bar Graph |

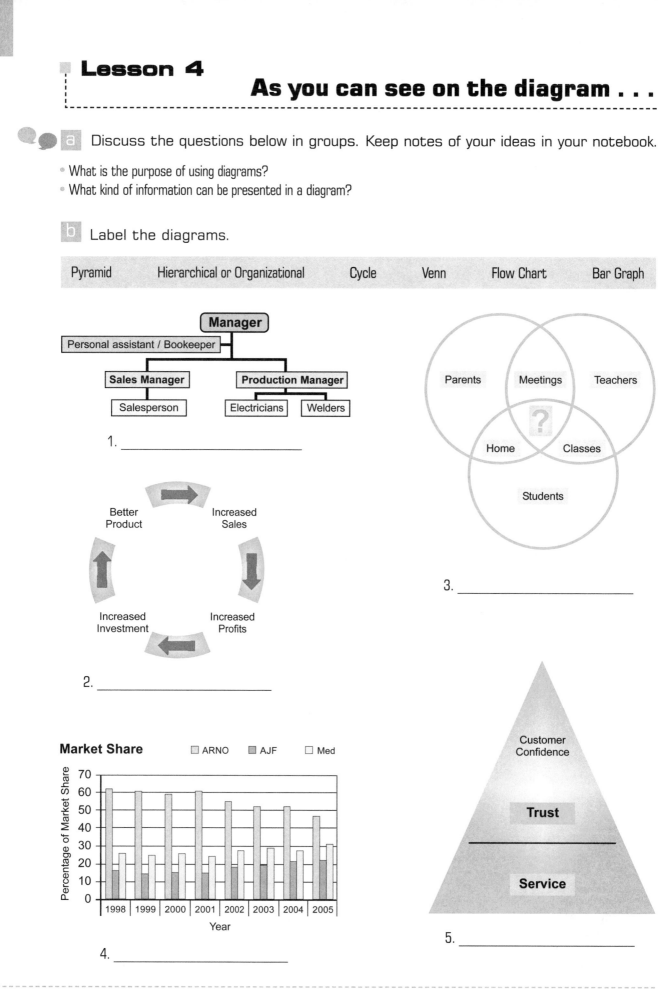

1. _____

2. _____

3. _____

4. _____

5. _____

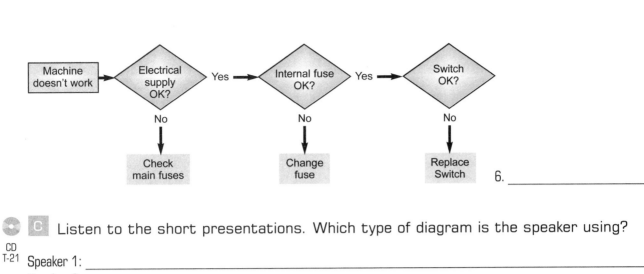

6. _____

c Listen to the short presentations. Which type of diagram is the speaker using?

CD T-21

Speaker 1: _____

Speaker 2: _____

Speaker 3: _____

Speaker 4: _____

Speaker 5: _____

Speaker 6: _____

d Listen again and underline the words or expressions that you hear.

CD T-21

Hierarchical or Organizational	**Cycle**	**Venn**
subordinate	leads to	common characteristics
assistant	circle	overlap
pecking order	return	coincide
level		circles
chain of command		

Pyramid	**Graph**	**Flow**
apex	vertical axis	decision
based on	horizontal axis	process
foundation	rise	flow
founded on	fall	branch
base	increase	diamond
	decrease	

e Which type of diagram would be useful to present the following information?

1. A production process _____
2. A computer program _____
3. Classification of the animal kingdom _____
4. The life cycle of a butterfly _____
5. The relationship between workers, management and clients _____
6. The effect of tax increases on profits _____

f Choose one of the topics in exercise **e** or a topic with which you are familiar, and make a suitable diagram that you could use as an aid in presenting your topic to the class.

Lesson 5

Thanks for coming to the meeting

a Match the moderating skills to the appropriate expressions.

Moderating Skills	Expressions
_____ 1. Open the meeting	a. Now, we need to specify some action points. OK, so would you write a report by next Thursday, please.
_____ 2. State objectives	b. OK, so to recap . . . So, the bottom line is . . .
_____ 3. Stimulate discussion	c. Shall we continue then? Just five more minutes so let's move along.
_____ 4. Clarify points	d. Thank you, but I think we are missing the point. I think we are digressing.
_____ 5. Keep discussion on topic	e. So, in other words, what you're saying is . . . Would you like to elaborate on that?
_____ 6. Control time	f. The purpose of this meeting is first to . . . and second to . . . The main objective of our meeting is . . .
_____ 7. Summarize	g. Well, ladies and gentleman, I think we should begin. Perhaps we'd better get down to business.
_____ 8. Organize further action	h. Would you like to add something here? What do other people think about this?

b Listen to and read the excerpt of a business meeting transcript.
Underline the statements that demonstrate good moderating skills.

CD
T-23

Walter: Ladies and gentlemen. Nice to see you all here. We're a little short on time so we'd better get down to business. A lot of our equipment is getting old so our first objective is to prioritize which equipment needs to be replaced. Second, our market share has fallen over the past four months and third, we have a very serious legal matter on our hands that I'd like Vincent de Nero to go over. If there is any other outstanding bussiness, we'll address it at the end, please.
Now our first point, we have 30 minutes to prioritize which equipment to replace. Jim, would you mind telling us what the priorities are in Radiography.

Jim: Sure. There is a great new scanner that has just come on to the market. We have to keep the department up-to-date, and I feel as though we need to buy one.

Walter: Fine, Jim, but I think you are missing the point. We are trying to identify *old* equipment that needs replacing.

Jim: Right! OK, the OPG machine is about 20 years old and is very unreliable. We are having to spend a lot of money on maintenance and half the time it doesn't work.

Walter: OK, so would you mind letting me know what it would cost to replace it, and send me three quotes by, let's say, next Friday. Now, Karen.

Karen: Thanks, Walter. OK, we're having a lot of problems with our Internet server. It seems our FWT computer terminals are not entirely compatible with their WSST language protocol. We're getting a lot of conflict error codes in the log.

Walter: So, what you are trying to say is that we either change the server or buy new computers.

Karen: Yeah. That's a pretty good summary.

c Work in groups of six. Pretend you are employees at ARNO and role-play the following meeting. At the end of the meeting, write your action points.

Topic	Time Limit	Objective	Action Points	Person	Deadline
Loss of market share	30 mins	To identify causes of market loss and develop a strategy and time line for reversing situation			

Student 1   Moderator

Tips
The meeting leader should facilitate and manage the meeting and not enter into the discussion.
Use the skills and language from exercise **a**.
Try to get everyone to agree.
If more information is needed, add this to the Action Points.

Market Share

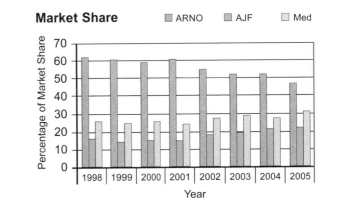

Students 2 and 3   Your views are:

Causes: Prices too high. Inefficient organization.
Strategies: Cut prices. Downsize workforce.
Employees should work overtime for free.
Reorganize management structure.
Invite an adviser to give recommendations.

Students 4 and 5   Your views are:

Causes: Old-fashioned image. Poor service.
Poor equipment.
Strategies: Training course for staff in improving services.
Modernize equipment. Launch advertising campaign.

Student 6   You are responsible for the minutes:

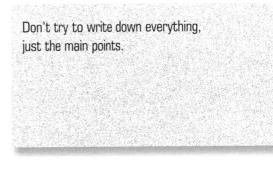

Don't try to write down everything, just the main points.

d Reflect on your work. Discuss how well you were able to meet your objectives, discuss points clearly and keep on task. Summarize your results. Then report your findings to the class.

Lesson 6

It's time to move on

a Check ✓ Yes or No in the chart. Discuss your answers in groups. Give reasons.

When you resign from a job, you should . . .	Yes	No
1. submit your resignation even if you don't have a job offer in writing.		
2. give a minimum of two weeks, resignation notice.		
3. criticize your company and / or its workers.		
4. ask for a letter of recommendation.		
5. say good-bye to your boss / bosses and co-workers.		
6. work until you leave.		
7. take home anything that is on your desk (pens, calculators, manuals, etc.).		
8. have your files in order.		

CD
T-24

b Listen to the conversations. Then discuss with a partner which conversation is more appropriate and why.

c Match the formal language with the informal language.

Formal - Written Language	Informal - Spoken Language
_____ 1. I intend to resign*.	a. OK, so I'm sorry.
_____ 2. I accept all responsibility.	b. Sure, I'll help the guy get started.
_____ 3. I regret my actions.	c. I'm going to quit*.
_____ 4. I regret having to inform you.	d. I messed up.
_____ 5. I am willing to train my replacement.	e. I'm sorry but you gotta know.

CD
T-25

d Listen to the final topic discussed in the meeting.
Complete the chart and decide who should resign.

Name	Error
shipping clerk, PHARMAQUIK	1.
warehouse staff, ARNO, Gerry	2.
nurse, Jenny Merton	3.

resign *v*	to choose to leave one's job or post
quit *v*	to leave, esp. a job; to stop doing

e A resignation letter contains the following points. Read the following resignation letter and underline the points.

- The purpose of the letter.
- Your regret in leaving the company.
- Positive comments about the company, co-workers, etc.
- Express gratitude for the opportunity to work there.

PHARMAQWIK
2405 Cactus Drive
Phoenix, AZ, 99065

January 02, 2006

Dear Wayne,

The purpose of this letter is to submit my resignation as shipping clerk. I would like to make this resignation effective as of Jan. 17, 2006. This should give you an opportunity to find a suitable replacement. Of course, I would be willing to provide training and orientation to my replacement.

The decision to leave PHARMAQWIK has not been an easy one. I regret leaving a stimulating and comfortable work environment. I also regret leaving all the good friends that I have made. However, I feel the change is necessary to pursue other interests and career goals.

I would like to reiterate that I will fulfill my obligations in the shipping and receiving department prior to my departure. In addition, I would like to make sure that the transition runs smoothly for everyone involved. This company has always been supportive and treated me and fairly. Also, I want to make sure that my co-workers don't have any problems. They have always worked hard and were good friends.

Working as part of your team has been a great learning experience. I would like to extent my gratitude to you and my co-workers for making this possible.

Sincerely,

Chung Lee

f In your notebook, write a letter of resignation. Remember to include the four points in exercise **e**.

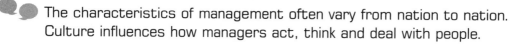

Team Project 5

The characteristics of management often vary from nation to nation. Culture influences how managers act, think and deal with people.

1. Brainstorm a list of products you could sell in a foreign market.

2. Where could you sell this product? You want to sell it in a country that is compatible with your country's culture. Brainstorm a list of possible target markets.

3. Select two foreign countries and search the web for their business styles and cultural differences. Write them in the chart. Share your findings with the class.

Example:

U.S.A.	Germany	Mexico
Managers communicate informally at work.	Managers have a strong sense of authority.	Managers normally do business at meals.
Americans use first names.	Managers are often older.	Managers are usually addressed by their titles.

Your country	Foreign Country 1	Foreign Country 2

Additional Resources

Review 1

A Complete the following contrary-to-fact sentences.

1. If I studied for an M.A. degree, _____*I'd have more professional opportunities.*_____
2. _____, I'd be updated.
3. _____, I would need computer skills.
4. If I saved up some money, _____
5. If I could choose a course for personal enrichment, _____
6. _____, I would apply for a job there.
7. _____, I would need to get a high score on the TOEFL.

B Complete the columns with advantages and disadvantages for each profesional development option.

	Advantages	Disadvantages
1. taking online courses		
2. studying for an M.A.		
3. working for a foreign company		
4. taking Continuing Education courses		
5. being reviewed by a supervisor		
6. studying abroad		

C Take turns answering the following questions. Then take a vote and choose the best answer.

If you were offered a 3-month job in another country, would you accept or reject it? Why?

Student A: I'd reject it. I wouldn't be able to adapt to their culture.

Student B: I'd accept it. I would probably learn a lot.

Student C: I'd accept it because I like challenges and new experiences.

1. If your teachers were asked to give you a reference, what would they probably say?
2. If you were an M.A. student abroad, would you return home to take modules online? Why?
3. If you were in another country for over a month, what would you miss the most?
4. Would you apply for a job to a multi-national company if you had the chance?
5. What kind of party would your classmates or co-workers organize for you if you were going to go away?

Review 2

A Brainstorm a list of qualities that companies look for when hiring personnel. Then complete the chart with the most adequate qualities for each position below.

Office Manager	Computer Technician	Environmental Engineer	Website Designer
_____	_____	_____	_____
_____	_____	_____	_____
_____	_____	_____	_____

B Order the parts of a cover letter by numbering them from 1-7.

____ request to meet with the employer   ____ reason for writing

____ your address   ____ formal greeting

____ formal closing   ____ company address

C Unscramble the questions and suggestions on how to dress for an interview. Remember to punctuate the sentence correctly.

1. wear / I / should / think / jacket / you / a

_____

2. conservative / better / be / wear / to / a / blouse / Wouldn't / it

_____

3. you / were / If / I / I / wear / wouldn't / so / jewelry / much

_____

4. suggest / Can / I / that / don't / you / put on / too / cologne / much

_____

5. Maybe / use / should / you / more / traditional / a / hairstyle

_____

D Use the cues below to write interview questions that an employer might ask you.

work experience	goals	effective team player	qualities	creative
skills and abilities	communication skills	greatest weakness		evaluate success
	contribute to our company			

A Unscramble and re-write the following questions. Then decide who would ask these questions and write L for landlord and T for tenant.

   _L_   1. monthly what you salary is   *What is your monthly salary?* _____

_____ 2. deposit I make need to a will? _____

_____ 3. the are you in ? apartment interested _____

_____ 4. lease? I for penalized would breaking the be _____

B Match the columns to make sentences.

_____ 1. Replacing an electric bulb is   a. respects your space and belongings.

_____ 2. I prefer living in a   b. allow them to have pets and plants in the house.

_____ 3. A good roommate is someone who   c. of all the expenses and maintenance it requires.

_____ 4. If I were a landlord, I'd   d. small house with a backyard.

_____ 5. I wouldn't like to live in a mansion because   e. easier than doing the laundry.

C Read the following ads and answer the questions.

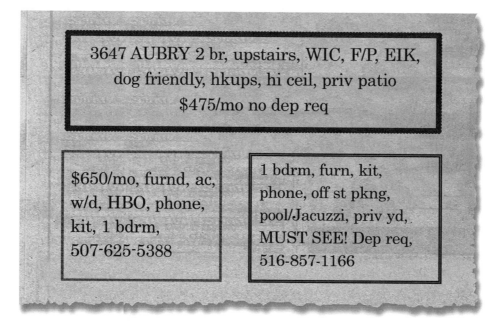

3647 AUBRY 2 br, upstairs, WIC, F/P, EIK,
dog friendly, hkups, hi ceil, priv patio
$475/mo no dep req

$650/mo, furnd, ac,
w/d, HBO, phone,
kit, 1 bdrm,
507-625-5388

1 bdrm, furn, kit,
phone, off st pkng,
pool/Jacuzzi, priv yd,
MUST SEE! Dep req,
516-857-1166

1. Which apartment is good for animal lovers? _____

2. Which apartment would be good if you don't not have enough money for a deposit? _____

3. Which apartment would be good for someone who likes to do exercise? _____

4. Which apartment would be good for someone who does not have furniture? _____

Review 4

A Complete the sentences with words from the box.

sales	figures	profits	advertising	budget	goals

1. Sales were better this year but we didn't improve _____ because we had to pay more taxes.
2. Old established companies do not need to invest much in _____ because they already have a good reputation.
3. What are your _____ for next year?
4. The current economic situation has affected our _____. They have decreased because people don't buy as much as they used to.
5. The company has a limited _____ for the Marketing Department. There are other priorities right now.

B Complete the sentences using *who, whose, where, that* or *which*.

1. I hate working with people _____ are stubborn.
2. I need a job _____ I make more money.
3. We need to hire people _____ experience is relevant for the job.
4. The company needs a person _____ has more experience in sales.
5. My office _____ is very small used to be the files room.
6. I used to have a teacher _____ classes were always interesting.

C Write sentences describing each graph using *used to*.

Taxes ▪ TAXES

1. *In 2004 the taxes **used to be** 13% now they are 15%*
2. _____

Employees ▪ EMPLOYEES

Exports ●─ EXPORTS

3. _____

4. _____

5. _____

Review 5

A Complete the crossword puzzle.

ACROSS

1. a list of topics to be covered in a meeting
3. items that are kept by a company for sale or use.
4. a written record of a meeting
6. items or goods made for sale at the retail level.
9. trouble, hassle
10. time or date by which something must be finished

DOWN

2. to send something
5. the person who leads or facilitates a meeting
7. get one's money back
8. a place

B Complete the conversation using the words and phrases from the box. Some words may be used more than once.

| why don't you | let's |
| how about | could |

Michelle: You heard about the visitors coming in on Friday, right?
Heidi: Yeah, what's going on?
Michelle: Well don't make any plans for the weekend.
Heidi: You mean we are going to have to entertain this weekend.
Michelle: That's right. So what do you suggest?
Heidi: Uhmmm . . . Maybe we (1) _____ take them out to dinner?
Michelle: I know that. I mean after dinner. What do we do?
Heidi: (2) _____ buying some tickets to the theater?
Michelle: But... don't you think it could be expensive.

Heidi: (3) _____ take them to a night club.
Michelle: No, it's too noisy.
Heidi: (4) _____ going to a basketball game. The Los Angeles Lakers are in town.
Michelle: That's expensive too!
Heidi: (5) _____ have a barbecue. It'll be fun, relaxing, and inexpensive.
Michelle: No thanks. I'm not going to cook this weekend.
Heidi: Hey! I got it.
Michelle: What! What!
Heidi: (6) _____ think of something to do? I'm all out of ideas.

C Circle the word or phrase that does not fit.

1. ship	send	dispatch	receive
2. stuff	hassle	quit	inconvenience
3. how about	hey	let's	why don't
4. agenda	chairperson	attendees	minute taker
5. pyramid	cycle	diagram	Venn
6. open the meeting	deadline	state objectives	stimulate discussion
7. leave	quit	apply	resign

Grammar Resource

Review: Adverbs of frequency

Examples	Explanation
Michael **always** rereads an exam paper before handing it in. He is **never** careless about his work. John **sometimes** studies in the library. Samantha **never** practices pronunciation.	Use the simple present tense with adverbs of frequency to show a regular activity.

Adverbs of frequency	always	100 %
	usually / generally	
	often / frequently	
	sometimes / occasionally	
	rarely / seldom / hardly ever	
	never / not ever	0 %

- Place the adverb of frequency after the verb *be*.
- Place the adverb of frequency before all other verbs.

ABOUT YOU Use adverbs of frequency and the words below to make statements that are true for you about your study and work habits.

1. punctual _____

2. late _____

3. careful _____

4. careless _____

5. creative _____

6. classes _____

7. notes _____

8. reports _____

9. deadlines _____

10. assignments _____

Contrary-to-fact conditionals: statements

Condition (*if* + subject + past tense verb)	Result (subject + *would* + verb)
If you **wanted** to get into a Masters program,	you **would have** to improve your grades.
If she **worked** harder,	she **would get** a promotion.
If I **weren't** so busy,	I **would get** a part time job.

- The *if* clause can come first or second in the sentence.
  *She would get a promotion **if she worked harder.***
- When the *if* clause comes first, use a comma between the two clauses.
- When the *if* clause comes second, no comma is needed.
- Use *were* for the past tense of *be* with all subjects in the *if* clause.

Note: Use contrary-to-the-fact conditionals to describe situations that are not true and you think will probably never be true.

PRACTICE

Fill in each blank with the correct tense of the verb in parentheses.

1. If tuition prices (be) __*were*__ lower, more students (go) __*would go*__ to graduate school.

2. If I (work) _____ harder, I (get) _____ better grades.

3. If he (be / not) _____ late every day, he (understand) _____ the lesson.

4. If I (have) _____ the money, I (take) _____ a vacation.

5. John (visit) _____ his parents more often if they (live) _____ closer.

6. I (do) _____ better on the listening test if the audio (be / not) _____ bad.

ABOUT YOU Use contrary-to-fact statements to say what you would do in these situations.

1. (win the lottery) _____

2. (get new computer)_____

3. (have a new car)_____

4. (win free plane ticket)_____

5. (make more money)_____

Contrary-to-fact conditionals: *Yes/no* questions

If + subject + past tense / would + subject + verb	Short answer
If you graduated this year, would you get a job?	Yes, I would. No, I wouldn't.
If she worked harder, would she get a promotion?	Yes, she would. No, she wouldn't.
If he weren't so busy, would he come to the movies?	Yes, he would. No, he wouldn't.

- The *if* clause can come first or second in the sentence.

  Would you get a part time job if you had more time?
- When the *if* clause comes first, use a comma between the two clauses.
- When the *if* clause comes second, no comma is needed.
- Use *were* for the past tense of *be* with all subjects in the *if* clause.

PRACTICE
Write a question using each statement.

1. If he made better grades, he would go to graduate school.

   _____

2. If she had a scholarship, she wouldn't have to work part time.

   _____

3. If I had a college degree, I would apply for a better job.

   _____

4. They would take a summer vacation if they had the money.

   _____

ABOUT YOU Complete the questions and answer them so they are true for you.

1. (pay an application fee) If I apply for an on-line course, _____

   _____

2. (get credit at school) If I took an on-line language course, _____

   _____

3. (get a better job) If I spoke three languages, _____

   _____

4. (quit part time job) If tuition were cheaper, _____

   _____

Contrary-to-fact conditionals: *Wh-* questions

If + subject + past tense / wh- word + would + subject + verb	Answer
If you **wanted** to get into a Masters program, **what would you do?** **If** she **needed** more money, **how would she get it?**	I **would** study harder. She **would** have to get another job.

- The *if* clause can come first or second in the sentence.
  - *What would she do **if she wanted the promotion?***
- When the *if* clause comes first, use a comma between the two clauses.
- When the *if* clause comes second, no comma is needed.
- Use *were* for the past tense of *be* with all subjects in the *if* clause.

PRACTICE

Complete each question using the information in parentheses.

1. If you _____ (can live) anywhere in the world, where _____
   _____ (live)?

2. If you _____ (finished school) this year, what _____
   _____ (do)?

3. Who _____ (ask) for advice if you _____ (want)
   to get a job?

4. How much money _____ (need) if you _____ (be)
   completely independent?

ABOUT YOU Answer the questions you completed in the exercise above with
complete statements that are true for you.

1. _____
2. _____
3. _____
4. _____
5. _____

Clauses with *because*

Main clause	Dependent clause
I want to work here	**because** the benefits are very good.
A full time job is not a good idea right now	**because** you are still in college.
This is a better option	**because** the hours are shorter and you can study on-line.

- *Because* is used with a dependent clause.
- A clause with *because* is not a complete sentence.
- If the sentence begins with the *because* clause, it is followed by a comma.

   Because he wants to finish college, *Sam is only working part time.*

Note: Connectors show the logical relationship between clauses in a sentence. A because clause answers the question: *Why?*

PRACTICE
Match the two columns below.

1. I need a part time job _____
2. The interviewer read my resume _____
3. This job opening won't last _____
4. I need a full time job _____
5. The interviewer never read my resume _____
6. No one is going to apply for this job _____

a. because the hours are really long.
b. because he was surprised I spoke French.
c. because the pay is great.
d. because I've just graduated.
e. because he knew all my hobbies.
f. because they've just increased our tuition.

ABOUT YOU Complete the sentences below with reasons that are true for you.

1. I am studying English _____

2. I plan / do not plan to continue my education _____

   _____

3. I would / wouldn't like to live in another country _____

   _____

4. I get / don't get very nervous before an interview _____

   _____

5. I am / am not happy with my life _____

   _____

Both . . . and / Neither . . . nor

First idea	Second idea	Statement of agreement
Susan thinks that hiring a new manager is the solution.	Mr. Jamison thinks that hiring a new manager is the solution.	**Both** Susan **and** Mr. Jamison **think** that hiring a new manager is the solution.
Frank doesn't like the new office site.	The construction boss doesn't like the new office site.	**Neither** Frank **nor** the construction boss **likes** the new office site.

- Use and in statements beginning with both.
- Use nor in statements beginning with neither.
- In a both/and statement, the verb agrees with the combined subject.
- In a neither/nor statement, the verb agrees with the second subject.

PRACTICE

Look at the chart. Write *True* or *False* in front of each statement.

	Ben	James	Paula	Marie
works part time	No	No	Yes	Yes
studies on-line	No	Yes	No	Yes
goes to college full time	Yes	No	Yes	No

1. _____ Neither Ben nor James has a job.

2. _____ Both Paula and Marie study on-line.

3. _____ Neither Ben nor Paula study on-line.

4. _____ Both James and Paula don't go to college.

5. _____ Neither James nor Marie goes to college full time.

ABOUT YOU Complete the chart with information that is true for you and two of your friends. Then using neither or both write statements about the information in the chart.

	Me		
works part time	____	____	____
studies on-line	____	____	____
goes to college full time	____	____	____

1. _____

2. _____

3. _____

4. _____

Review: Present perfect

	Subject + *has/have* + past participle
Affirmative statement	**He has gone** to three job interviews. Subject + *has/have* + *not/never* + past participle
Negative statement	**I have never gone** to a job interview. *Has/have* + subject + past participle
Yes/no question	**Have you heard** from the hiring manager yet? *Wh-* word + *has/have* + subject + past participle
Wh- question	**How long has he worked** at ECCM publishers?

Note: Use the present perfect in the following situations:
   a. to show that something happened at an unspecified time in the past;
   b. to show that something happened more than once in the past; or
   c. to show that something started at a specific time in the past and continues in the present.

PRACTICE

Complete each sentence with the correct present perfect form of the verb in parentheses.

1. (be) Michael _____ looking for a job for three weeks.

2. (go) He _____ to four different interviews.

3. (not / wear) I think he _____ the right clothes to these interviews.

4. (not / sleep) He's also very nervous. And _____ well for days.

5. (hear) (you) _____ about any good job openings lately?

ABOUT YOU Using the words in parentheses write present perfect questions. Then answer them in complete sentences with information that is true for you.

1. Q: (you / ever / go / on / job interview) _____
   A: _____

2. Q: (you / write / your / resume) _____
   A: _____

3. Q: (how long / you / be / university _____
   A: _____

Review: Verb + gerund form vs. verb + infinitive form

Example	Explanation
I like **working** in an office. I like **to work** in an office.	Some verbs can be followed by either a gerund or an infinitive with no difference in meaning.
I stopped **eating** lunch at noon. I stopped **to eat** lunch at noon.	After the verbs *stop, remember, forget*, and *try* the meaning of a gerund is different than the meaning of an infinitive.
<ul><li>Only use a gerund after the verbs enjoy, finish, give up, dislike.</li><li>Only use an infinitive after the verbs want, plan, decide, would like.</li></ul>	

PRACTICE
Match the sentences that have the same meaning.

1. _____ He continued studying after he got a job.
2. _____ She stopped to have some coffee after work.
3. _____ I didn't remember to check my messages.
4. _____ He started studying after he got a job.
5. _____ She stopped having coffee after work.
6. _____ I didn't remember checking my messages.

a. I checked my messages, but forgot I did it.
b. He didn't stop studying after he got a job.
c. She had coffee after work.
d. He didn't study until after he got a job.
e. She no longer drinks coffee after work.
f. I forgot to check my messages.

ABOUT YOU   Rewrite the sentence with the correct infinitive or gerund to make a true statement about you.

1. Once I get a job I plan to (continue to study / start studying).

_____

2. In class I (always / never) stop (to pay / paying) attention after five minutes.

_____

3. I usually remember (to do / doing) my homework after any class.

_____

4. I never forget (to hand in / handing in) an assignment before the deadline.

_____

Comparative form of adjectives

Type of adjective	Simple form	Comparative form
One-syllable adjectives	dark	dark**er**
One-syllable adjectives ending in -e	nice	nice**r**
One-syllable adjectives ending in consonant-vowel-consonant	small	small**er**
Two-syllable adjectives	modern	**more** modern
Two-syllable adjectives ending in -y	lively	livel**ier**
Some two syllable adjectives that have two forms	quiet friendly	quiet**er** or **more** quiet friendl**ier** or **more** friendly
Adjectives with three or more syllables	expensive	**more** expensive

- Use the comparative form to compare two things.
- If the second item is mentioned in the sentence, use than before it.

    *This apartment is **bigger than** yours.*

PRACTICE

Write the comparative form of these adjectives.

1. close_____
2. noisy_____
3. comfortable_____
4. big _____
5. beautiful_____

6. quiet_____
7. ugly_____
8. clean_____
9. spacious_____
10 convenient_____

ABOUT YOU Complete the sentences below with reasons that are true for you.

1. (expensive) _____
2. (comfortable) _____
3. (modern) _____
4. (beautiful garden) _____
5. (technological features) _____

Causative verbs

Subject + causative verb + indirect object + verb	Explanation
I **had a locksmith change** all the locks before I moved in.	*Have* means to give a job or a task to someone.
The landlord **makes us keep** our bikes inside the apartment.	*Make* means to force or require.
But he does **let the kids roller blade** in the patio.	*Let* means to permit.
The lease **allows tenants to make** improvements to the apartment.	*Allow* means to permit.

Note: *Have, make, let* and *allow* are called causative verbs because they show that one person causes another to do something.

Review: Causative with *get*

Subject	+ (modal)	+ (adverb)	+ get	+ direct object	+ past participle	
I	need to		**get**	the bathroom	fixed.	
We		just	**got**	the windows	washed	yesterday.
The landlord			**will get**	the leaky roof	fixed	this month.

- Any tense of the verb *get* can be used as a causative verb.

Note: A causative verb shows that the subject causes something to happen.

PRACTICE
Unscramble the words to make sentences.

1. patios / keep / clean / the / makes / all / landlord / his / tenants / the

   _____

2. Stephen / change / had / faucet / the / old / plumber / a

   _____

3. everyone / has / the / sign / a lease/ landlord

   _____

4. the landlord / I / get / have to / to fix / bathroom / this

   _____

ABOUT YOU   Write two sentences to describe things you would get changed or repaired before moving into a new apartment.

_____

_____

Used to

Example	Explanation
Our company **used to** have 13,000 employees.	*Used to* + a base form shows a habit or custom over a past period of time.
Richmond Tobacco **did not use to** produce menthol cigarettes.	For negatives, omit the *-d* in *used to*.

Note: Used to *is* for past habits or customs.
It is not for an action that happened once or a few times.

PRACTICE

Fill in the first blank in each sentence with the affirmative or negative form of used to and the verb in parentheses. Fill in the second blank with the present tense of the verb in parentheses.

1. Mr. Chen _____ (work) in marketing; he _____ (be) now in sales.

2. Margaret _____ (not be) Ben's assistant; but now she _____ (be).

3. We _____ (have) five warehouses, but now ARCO _____ (store) our products for us.

4. Employees _____ (not speak) English, but now the company _____ (make) everyone speak two languages.

ABOUT YOU Write sentences comparing the way your life has changed as a university student or professional.

1. live with my family _____

_____

2. watch a lot of TV _____

_____

3. work forty hours a week _____

_____

4. go to the gym _____

_____

5. spend a lot of time with my friends _____

_____

Modals for suggestions, advice, and necessity

Modal	Example	Use
could	Marion **could** work full time.	Suggestion
should shouldn't	We **should** get management training. He **shouldn't** work so much overtime.	Advice
have to not have to	This department **has to** increase productivity. You **don't have to** hire more staff.	Necessity
need to not need to	He **needs to** set concrete goals. That equipment **doesn't need to** be repaired.	Necessity

- Always use a base verb after a modal (could and should).
- Modals never take -s, -ed, and -ing endings.
- Verb phrases used as modals do take -s, -ed, and -ing endings.

Note: *Have to* and *need to* are expressions that have same meaning as modals.

PRACTICE
Answer each question with a complete sentence.

1. Does he need to save money? (NO) _____

2. Should he get more training? (YES) _____

3. Don't you have to be at a meeting (NO) _____

4. Should she ask someone for help? (YES) _____

5. Don't they need to manage their time? (YES) _____

 **ABOUT YOU** Answer these questions with true statements about you.

1. Do you need to study harder?

_____

2. Should you get a part time job?

_____

3. Do you have to learn to manage your time to meet deadlines?

_____

4. Do you need someone to give you advice about job hunting?

_____

Adjective clauses *that, which,* and *where*

	Main clause	**adjective clause**
Subject clause	This is the course	**that (which)** will make a difference in your performance.
	The company	**where** I work has a great retirement program.
Object clause	I like the new copier	**that (which)** they just bought.

- An adjective clause is a group of words that describe the preceding noun.
- *That, which,* and *where* are relative pronouns.
- Relative pronouns connect the main clause to the adjective clause.

PRACTICE
Use adjective clauses to combine two sentences.

1. The parking lot is a block away. I left my car there.

   _____

2. The company is closing down. They make our computers.

   _____

3. The parts are very expensive. We need the parts to fix our equipment.

   _____

4. The sales goal was not met. We set the sales goal last year.

   _____

5. We used to sell other products last year. The other products were not popular.

   _____

6. The companies are letting chemical residues into the river. These residues are very toxic.

   _____

7. The employees have been wasting time. They need the time to increase productivity.

   _____

8. If the numbers don't improve, the company will close down. The sales force promised the numbers.

   _____

Adjective clauses with *who*, *whom*, and *whose*

	Main clause	**adjective clause**
Subject clause	Mr. Shibuya is the boss	**who (that)** has influenced me the most.
	I have a manager	**whose** goal statements are always motivating.
Object clause	The managerial candidate	**whom (who)** I met today seems perfect.
	The manager	**for whom** you work is essential to your growth.
	The management trainer	**whose** course we took had worked here before.

- Use *whose* for possession as a substitute for *his, her, its, their,* or a possessive noun.
- In formal English, a preposition comes before the relative pronoun in an object clause.

Note: In spoken English *who* often substitutes *whom* in the object clause.

PRACTICE
Complete the sentences using *who, whom,* or *whose.*

1. Mr. Perez is the kind of manager to _____ you can tell all your problems.

2. The supervisor _____ came last week was very efficient.

3. I prefer managers _____ goals are realistic.

4. I have four employees _____ work habits need to be improved.

5. The manager _____ I most admire left last year.

6. The people _____ I have met at this company are all very loyal.

ABOUT YOU Complete the sentences below so they are true about you.

1. The person whom I most admire _____

_____

2. The people who work with me _____

_____

3. The students who I used to study with _____

_____

4. The professor whose class I most enjoyed _____

_____

Embedded questions: *Wh-* questions

Wh- question	Introductory question	Embedded question
Where are the invoices?	Can you show me	**where** the invoices **are**?
Who is the new manager?	Do you know	**who** the new manager **is**?
When does our meeting start?	I forgot	**when** our meeting **starts**.

- In an embedded *wh-* question, the subject comes before the verb.
- The auxiliaries *do / does* are not used in embedded questions.

Note: An embedded question is a question that is placed inside another question or statement. We use embedded questions to make questions more polite.

PRACTICE

Find the *wh-* question in each embedded question.

1. Will you show me where the warehouse is?   *Where's the warehouse?*

2. Could you explain what the reporting process is?   _____

3. Do you know who orders office supplies?   _____

4. Can you show me how to work the photocopier?   _____

5. Can you tell me when the orders are arriving?   _____

ABOUT YOU   Use some of the expressions in the box to write embedded questions about these aspects of your life.

> Can you . . .   Will you . . .   Do you know . . . .
>   Do you have any idea . . .   I forgot . . .

1. classes _____

2. textbooks _____

3. reports _____

4. deadlines _____

5. assignments _____

Glossary

A

accounting *n, adj*	the profession of a person who keeps records of a company's finances
achieve *v*	to reach, to gain
agenda *n*	a list of topics to be covered in a meeting
arbitrator *n*	mediator, judge
asset *n*	an advantage, a benefit
availability *n*	free to start work

B

back order *n*	a delayed order due to item not being in stock
brewing *n, adj*	making beer
budget *n*	an amount of money set aside for a specific purpose

C

campaign *n*	an organized effort by people to reach a goal
chairperson *n*	the person who leads or facilitates a meeting
circulate *v*	to distribute
competitor *n*	a product or company that competes with others for the same customers
complementary *adj*	positive, praising
credit *n*	a unit of a course at a school, university or college

D

deadline *n*	a time or date by which something must be finished
deal with *v*	to interact with someone
deliver *n*	to give, to pass on
dispatch *v*	send it, send it off, get it off
downsize *v*	to reduce the number of employees in a company
drop off *v*	leave
drum *n*	a barrel made from metal
duties *n*	obligations, responsibilities

F

fee *n*	charge, cost

G

goal *n*	an objective, a purpose

H

head *v*	to go to

I

image *n*   a company or a person's appearance to others

implement *v*   to start, to put in to action

improve *v*   to make something better

income *n*   money earned from working or investment

inconvenience *n*   trouble, hassle

iodine *n*   a brownish-orange chemical element used in medicine

K

knowledgeable *adj*   to have information on or familiarity with something

L

landlord *n*   a person who owns a house, apartment, or room that people can rent

lawsuit *n*   a legal action bringing a claim to a court of law

lead *v*   to direct, to control

lecture *n*   a speech on a topic usually at a university

long term *adj*   extending over a long period of time

loyalty *n*   faithfulness, devotion, allegiance

M

maintenance *n*   keep equipment, machinery in good working order

management *n*   the art and science of directing a business

measurable *adj*   the ability to measure something

merchandise *n*   items, goods made for sale at the retail level

minutes *n*   a written record of the meeting

O

observable *adj*   the ability to observe something

optimize *v*   to get the best outcome possible

P

persistent *adj*   someone who perseveres, never quits

procedure *n*   detailed steps for doing something

proficiency *n*   ability to work with skill, expertise

profile *n*   a group of characteristics

profit *n*   money remaining after business expenses are deducted

pushy *adj*   aggressive, too demanding of the attention and cooperation of others

Q

quit *v*   to leave, esp. a job

R

raw material *n*   basic material needed to manufacture something
realistic *adj*   based on reality, not on something which is unlikely to happen
refund *v*   get one's money back
remuneration *n*   payment for doing something, salary
resign *v*   to choose to leave one's job
resignation *n*   the act of choosing to leave one's post
restricted *adj*   limited in use in availability
retirement *n*   stopping work due to age or poor health

S

scholarship *n*   a grant to pay for study
settle *v*   to come to an agreement
shift *n*   a segment of work time
ship *v*   to send something
stock *n*   items that are kept by a company for sale or use

T

take delivery of *v*   receive, get
training *n*   a process of education, instruction
tuition *n*   school fee
tutorial *n*   classes given to individual students

U

up-to-date *adj*   modern, state of the art

V

venue *n*   a place

W

workforce *n*   all employed workers in a company

Audio Script

Lesson 1

CD T-1

Takeshi: You know what? Trying to describe your personal feelings about yourself is very hard to do.

Paula: What do you mean?

Takeshi: Well, for this job application I had to answer a test about myself before I went into the interview. It was full of statements about how I react or think I react in different situations. I could only answer with Always, Sometimes, Never, and Not sure. It makes you feel that there is only one right answer.

The first question was about being a leader. I guess I am to a certain extent, so I put a check next to Sometimes.

Paula: I agree with you about that.

Takeshi: Then the second question was about getting things done well. Everyone I know complains that I'm a perfectionist so I said "Always" to that one. Then the next one was about making decisions with your emotions. I think I use my head but I answered "Not sure."

Paula: Hmmm. I'm not quite sure I agree with either answer, but don't stop.

Takeshi: Do you think I'm an active person because I marked off that I was - always.

Paula: Yes, I think you are really active.

Takeshi: And what do you think? Am I pushy?

Paula: If what you mean is aggressive, then you are not at all.

Takeshi: Great because that's exactly what I answered.

Paula: Hey, I think you answered what other people think about you and not what you think about yourself.

Lesson 5

CD T-2

RECORDING: Welcome to Country University. Dial the number if you know the extension. If you do not know the extension listen to the following instructions. Dial one for Continuing Education information. Dial two for Distance Education information. Dial four for Master Degree information. Dial zero to speak to an assistant. Thank you for calling the undergraduate department.

Lesson 6

CD T-3

Mrs. Jackson: Good morning, Paula. How's life treating you?

Paula: Fine, thanks, Mrs. Jackson.

Mrs. Jackson: OK, so we're going to go through your first review. The first thing I want is for you to reflect on your own performance so far. What do you see as your strengths - what have been your strong points?

Paula: OK. I think I'm coping with the new environment. It's very different from studying in my country. I'm working hard and getting my assignments in on time. I don't know what else. It's hard to see your own good points.

Mrs. Jackson: Right! But you're doing fine. Tell me, how do you get on with the other students? Are you making friends?

Paula: Mhm, not many. I'm not very outgoing and I find it difficult to make new friends here. Everyone is so busy; they don't have time for other people. I really miss my friends back home.

Mrs. Jackson: And are you happy with the grades you're getting?

Paula: No, not really. I had to rewrite two assignments. I was very disappointed with the result. Writing academic papers in English is harder than I imagined. I just can't organize my ideas logically. I need to work on this. Unfortunately, I don't know exactly what to do to improve.

Mrs. Jackson: That's a good observation. We've noticed that as well. There are a couple of other things your teachers have noticed and commented on. First, you don't take part in class discussions. It's very important to join in; you'll get more from the course and it could help you to make friends as well.

Paula: That's a fair comment. OK, I know I can work on that.

Mrs. Jackson: And the other thing is that you have to spend more time reading. You're assignments need more theory --- a stronger basis for your arguments. Your own comments are valuable, but you have to support these.

Paula: Oh, I see. The problem is that I work in the library for four hours a day, and at the end of the shift, I'm tired of the entire atmosphere and I just don't feel like staying there to study.

Mrs. Jackson: OK, we all need a bit more money. New York's not cheap, is it? But anyway, we now need to think about exactly what you're going to do to improve. We need a few concrete goals and an action plan with a calendar.

Unit 2   Getting the Job

Lesson 1

CD T-4

Art: Good, everyone's here now. There's fresh coffee if anybody wants some. OK. Let's start, please. As you all know, we are trying to find the right person, with the right qualifications for each position currently available in the company. OK. First on the list: Two experienced architects with lots of energy and confidence. They have to have communication and leadership skills.

Norma: How much experience are you asking for? 3? 5 years?

Art: At least four years experience.

Norma: OK.

Art: We also need five experienced construction workers. Teamwork skills are essential here. We'd also like to see dedication and perseverance in our construction workers.
And also. The company is looking for an administrator. The candidate needs an excellent professional appearance as he or she will be reporting to the City Construction Board; top on the list of qualifications: problem-solving skills, and last but not least, honesty and integrity. Is that all, Norma?

Norma: Yes, that's it.

Art: Please guys keep in mind all the required qualifications for each position available. Thank you very much for coming.

Lesson 3

CD T-5

Tim, the hiring manager, is looking over some recent applications for a job opening in the import/export department when Gunther, the personnel assistant, walks into his office

Gunther: Hi, Tim. How's everything going?

Tim: Oh, not too bad. Just looking over some cover notes and resumes for a vacant post.

Gunther: Oh yeah? What department?

Tim: The import /export department. We need a new manager there.

Gunther: But, isn't Chantal Zidane the manager?

Tim: Haven't you heard? She just applied for early retirement.

Gunther: You're kidding!

Tim: No . . . I'm not.   She has a medical condition that needs to be taken care of.

Gunther: Wow . . . That's too bad . . . So . . . any good candidates for the import/export manager position?

Tim: Well . . . as a matter of fact there's this one. Here, I have an extra copy.

Lesson 3

CD T-6

Gunther: Let's see . . . Scarlet Louise Collier . . . 1206 South Magnolia Avenue

Tim: No, no, no . . . 1206 South Magnolia Street in Anchorage, Alaska. Look where she went to school!

Gunther: Nice! She has a law degree from the University of Stanford! And a PhD in International Business from Notre Dame University.

Gunther: Hey . . . I'm impressed -- she's bar certified in two states.

Tim: Yeah . . . Washington and California . . . and she has computer skills as well as excellent oral communication skills.

Gunther: Well . . . I'm convinced. Is there anything else we need to know?

Tim: Well, she's presently working at ANPETROL as an attorney. She needs to give a two week notice.

Gunther: Why does she want to leave the company?

Tim: Well . . . she would like to be closer to her children who live in Washington.

Gunther: When she worked at EXPRESS HR SERVICES. She was responsible for all labor contract negotiations there.

Tim: Well. . . negotiating labor contracts can be a headache.

Gunther: Yeah, I guess so. You know, her resume is quite impressive. She's even worked as an import/export assistant at BLUE POINT AUTO. Doesn't say why she left, however.

Tim: No it doesn't, but we can call Carlos Fernandez Díaz, her supervisor.

Gunther: The name is Carlos FERNANDO Díaz.

Tim: Hey, you're right. It does say Carlos Fernando Díaz.

Lesson 6

Mr. Weasley: Good morning, Ms. Edwards. Please have a seat.

Ms. Edwards: Good morning.

Mr. Weasley: [paper rustles] Thank you for coming to the interview. Well, I see on your resume that you have experience in marketing. Can you tell me more about your job at University Radio?

Ms. Edwards: I worked at University Radio for two years. I was in charge of the marketing department. I had several key responsibilities. During the time I was there, I modified several marketing procedures in order to make them more efficient. By implementing these modifications, I increased sales by 10% over a two year period. Of course, I had to train my marketing team so they could carry out the new procedures for market studies and customer service. So, basically, I modified processes, I implemented change, I increased sales and I trained my sales team.

Mr. Weasley: I see, and why did you decide to leave?

Ms. Edwards: Well, unfortunately . . .

Unit 3 Relocating for work

Lesson 1

CD T-9

Fernanda: How are you finding New York? It must be very different from Germany

Cordula: Well, I 'm from Munich. Living in a beautiful city like Munich is very enjoyable. New York is so noisy and busy. But I like the people here. They are friendly to foreigners. Life in New York seems freer and more open too.

Fernanda: Is Germany expensive?

Cordula: Yes! Especially if you rent a house or an apartment. They are really expensive. How about

Mexico? It must be a lot quieter than New York.

Fernanda: It sure is, but I like New York. Life is much more exciting here than in Mexico. I just find it harder to meet people here. Mexicans are much friendlier than New Yorkers.

Cordula: Really, sounds like a great place. What about the cost of housing in Mexico? Is it expensive?

Fernanda: Well..houses or apartments in middle-class areas are not easy to find and rent is usually between 500 and 650 dollars a month.

Cordula: That's not such a bad deal. You'd have to pay twice as much in Munich. What about here in New York ? Is it much more expensive than in Mexico?

Fernanda: Definitely.

Cordula: OK, I know where I'm going to spend my next vacation.

Lesson 3

CD T-10

Fernanda: How's the apartment hunting going?

Cordula: Oh, it's really slow.

Fernanda: What's the problem?

Cordula: Well the big problem is to find somewhere that suits me and is OK for my husband and daughter as well. There's so much to consider.

Fernanda: So what would be your perfect apartment?

Cordula: Well, the only thing that is important for me is that I would like to be near work. I don't want to spend a lot of time traveling to and from work.

Fernanda: Yeah, who does?

Cordula: But then my husband - he's an artist you know - well, he wants somewhere that has a lot of natural light. And then he doesn't like American food, so we won't be eating in restaurants very often. He wants a nice big kitchen where he can cook Indian food.

Fernanda: And he wants to be near the galleries as well I suppose.

Cordula: Of course! And then there's my daughter. We have this dog that she really loves and we promised that we would let her bring the dog with us.
Have you ever tried to find an apartment that allows pets, is near the galleries and school and . . .

Fernanda: OK, OK I see what you mean! Well at least you don't have to worry too much about the cost because the company is going to pay 50% of your rent.

Cordula: Yeah, we got a good deal there.

Lesson 4

CD
T-11

Radio host: Good morning. This is Radio XRTB. The Johnny Fernandez' Morning Show. Today we have something a little different. Visiting us is Emily Parks, a broker at The Avenue Real Estate Company. Emily is here today to give all the potential tenants in our audience some expert advice on apartment hunting. Emily, what exactly do you have to do to find a good apartment.

Broker: Well, the search starts by collecting every newspaper, and rental brochure published in your city. It's also a good idea to check out all the bulletin boards and advertising kiosks in the neighborhoods where you would like to live. Many good apartments are never advertised in newspapers.
Next step, the telephone. Call the number for every ad you see that looks like it could be right.
You're going to be making dozens of calls and leaving as many messages.

Radio host: I see where I went wrong already. I only called the number of apartments I thought I could see in a day.

Broker: Oh, no! You'll never find an apartment that way. A lot of the apartments are not going to be right for you. Many of them will already be rented. And some people will not return your call. So you have to make at least 20 calls every day. And if you left a message and no one returns it, call them again the following day. But remember: be tactful.

Radio host: Yeah, no one likes to be pressured.

Broker: And once you've started the actual search, once you're out there looking at apartments, keep your checkbook with you. When you see an apartment you like, do not hesitate and act upon it quickly.
Good places do not stay on the market long! Often, people lose good places due to indecision.

Radio host: I'm sure you're right about that, Emily. But what about papers? What if the landlord asks you for a credit report. Isn't that important?

Broker: It certainly is. You need all your paperwork together before you visit your first apartment. Not every landlord asks for a credit report, but they all like tenants who are organized and prepared.

Radio host: Anything else we need to know before we run out of time?

Broker: Yes. Think of your first meeting with the landlord as a job interview. Dress and groom properly.

Landlords of really good units are looking for someone able and responsible enough to pay rent on time and who will treat them and their property with care and respect.
And last of all, once you've made an appointment, do show up and never be late. No-shows are evidence of irresponsibility and the majority of the building managers and landlords hate irresponsible tenants.
So be optimistic! Finding a great place can be daunting, but it is well worth the effort.

Radio host: Thank you, Emily.

Lesson 5

CD
T-12

Fernanda: Hi, Cordula, how's the apartment hunting going?

Cordula: Oh, don't ask!

Fernanda: What's the problem?

Cordula: Well, I've been looking at lofts. My husband likes the idea of a loft.

Fernanda: Why?

Cordula: I don't know. They're fashionable at the moment and they do appear to have more space than an ordinary apartment.

Fernanda: How is that?

Cordula: Well, they usually have higher ceilings and the bedroom is above the living room.

Fernanda: So, what's the problem?

Cordula: Well, first, they're really expensive.

Fernanda: What isn't!

Cordula: Right! And second, they are really difficult to find because everybody wants one. I phone up as soon as I see the advert - and it's already gone.

Fernanda: Now that must be frustrating.

Cordula: And then all the agencies and landlords are using the word "loft" even to describe regular apartments. I wasted a whole afternoon going to see a so-called loft. When I found the place it was just a one room box.

Fernanda: I see what you mean.

Cordula: And then there are all these abbreviations in the newspapers.

Fernanda: Yeah, all that immac. cond. and W.I.C. stuff.

Cordula: That's right. Those abbreviations drive me crazy.

Lesson 6

Conversation 1

CD T-13

A: Home repair. May I help you?

B: Hi. Could you send a technician over, please?

A: Of course ma'am, what kind of problem do you have?

B: There's water everywhere! Please hurry! The kitchen is all flooded!

A: Don't worry ma'am, but what exactly is the problem?

B: If I only knew! It has to be either the faucet or the sink! I just got back from vacation. I don't know what the problem is. Please, help!

A: Ok, ok ma'am. Take it easy. We'll be right there as soon as we can. Tell me your address, please.

B: It's Marble Street . . .

Conversation 2

A: Light up your life, How may I help you?

B: CUSTOMER: My lights have gone out. I can't see a thing.

A: What?

B: CUSTOMER: No, no, no. The power is out. I'm new in town and I don't know what to do.

A: Oh I see. Do your neighbors have any power?

B: CUSTOMER: No, ma 'am. The whole street's dark. I'm in the Shine area, downtown.

A: Don't worry, ma 'am. It's a small blackout. The city electricians are taking care of it. It's a matter of . . .

B: CUSTOMER: Wait. The power is on now. Thanks.

A: At your service, ma'am. Light up your life is pleased to help you. Thanks for calling.

Conversation 3

A: Hello. I'm calling about the ad in the newspaper. I'm having some problems with my doors.

B: Yes, sir. And what seems to be the problem?

A: They don't seem to fit properly.

B: Why? What's wrong with them?

A: I think they must be rubbing against the floor. Every morning there's dust under them. Sometimes I sweep it up to three times a day.

B: Mmm. I think you've got termites.

A: Oh no! Can you come and exterminate them?

B: No, sir. We just do the woodwork. But if you like I can send you someone to have a look. What's the address? . . .

Unit 4 Doing the Job

Lesson 1

CD T-14

Mr. Kourchenko: The job of a CEO is to see the big picture, to set long term goals, and design strategies that will ensure the company's future long term success. Red Klover Beer, I believe, is a company with a great future.

I've already spent some time reviewing the company's present position and I have come to the conclusion that within 5 years, the company should be able increase its domestic market share by 20%. I would also like to see Red Klover entering the Asian market where I believe there is great potential. Now let me move from the long term goals to the short term goals First of all, we need to deal with the short term financial problem that the company is facing. We need to examine the problem in detail and identify the causes of this problem. Then we need to set some careful short term goals and to develop concrete action plans in order to regain our position in the market and overcome these financial difficulties. So, my first step will be to have a meeting with the heads of departments to spell out the problem and identify goals. They will then each delineate the proper action plans for their departments.

In spite of the problem the company has had recently, I am confident that Red Klover Beer's future is bright. However, we need to work really hard and come up with creative solutions that allow us to deal with the current situation. Teamwork will be essential to work things out and achieve our objectives. I have total confidence in the capacity of the management team. However, if managers do not reach their goals in time, then I will not hesitate in retrenching them.

Lesson 2

CD T-15

Mr. Kourchenko: OK, we all know the basic problem - profits are down. Now we have to identify the cause of the problem. I have analyzed the figures for the last five years and it is clear that there are two main causes: high production costs and poor sales.

If you look at this graph, you will see that the unit production costs were .75☐ two years ago and now they are .96☐. This is just not competitive.

Mr. Shibuya: The problem is that the machinery we have is getting old. We have to stop the production line to repair machines and this severely affects our production costs.

Mr. Kourchenko: Do we have a maintenance program for the machines?

Mr. Shibuya: Er, no. We just fix the machines when they break down.

Mr. Kourchenko: OK. Looks like there's a plan just being asked to be implemented! Get to it! Now let us turn to sales. As you can see in the next graph, during the last year our annual sales have decreased 18%. That's down to 6,500,000€ in revenue.

Ms. Parks: Excuse me, can you please be more specific? You said 6'500,000€, but how much did we use to sell before last year?

Mr. Kourchenko: Sure, we had annual sales of 8,000,000€, hence the 18% decrease I just mentioned. So what are the causes of these low sales? I've identified four different problem areas: strong foreign competition, a reduced advertising budget, limited number of products and special offers. Let's start with the competitors. As you all know, the number of competitors has increased due to the free trade agreements with Germany, Austria and Mexico. When we started this business we used to have four competitors; now we have seven. This strong competition has forced us to start a new product development project. You all know that the company decided to launch a new beer to offer five products instead of four. Unfortunately, we were forced to withdraw the new product because of its low impact on the market.

There wasn't any appropriate field research, so we didn't gain any competitive advantage in the marketplace. This lack of success has affected our sales dramatically.

Ms. Edwards: Is that decrease in sales also related to the fact that this year we had only two campaigns for special offers?

Mr. Kourchenko: Absolutely. Reports from the past indicate that we used to have an average of three special campaigns per year, but this year there were only two. Why? Because there was a reduction in the advertising budget.

Mr. Shibuya: Excuse me, can you explain why the advertising budget was reduced if we needed to increase sales?

Mr. Kourchenko: Good question, Mr. Shibuya! As you can imagine, the company invested a great deal of money in the new product development and its specific advertising campaign. Since the product didn't have good acceptance in the market, all that investment affected the company's cash flow and the annual budget suffered as you can see from this graph. We used to assign 14% to advertising, but we were forced to reduce to 10% this year. The reduction definitely played a major part in the drop in annual sales.

Ms. Parks: I see, so the advertising budget decreased by 4% from 14 in the previous year to 10% in the current year?

Mr. Kourchenko: That's correct. And, well, as a consequence, our profits have also been severely affected. This other graph shows how we had made an average of 40% profit a year, while the yearly report from this year shows profits of 35%.

Ms. Parks: Umm, sorry to interrupt again. Did you say from 40 to 35%?

Mr. Kourchenko: Yes, I'm afraid so. And well, to sum up, all these figures show that our current financial situation does not look good.

Lesson 4

CD T-16

Ms. McCartney: No, we can't sack Jim. He's been here for years. In fact he's been here since the company was started. He knows so much about the company.

Mr. Kourchenko: True, but performance is what it's all about and the Marketing Department has not been performing very well.

Ms. McCartney: But everyone really respects him, he's like a father to us all. I can't imagine Red Klover without Jim.

Mr. Kourchenko: But we are making a business decision here. We mustn't let personal sentiments affect business decisions. Look at his performance over the last few years. The Diet Draught was a big failure. It cost the company millions and it was all because the market research was poorly done.

Ms. McCartney: But Jim has had some great successes in the past. He was the one who introduced our top selling product, MixIt, to the market and look how much money that has made.

Mr. Kourchenko: True, but that was in the past. We can't live in the past. In the business, you are only as good as your last product. And his last product was a disaster.

Ms. McCartney: But surely, stability is important in a management team. If we keep changing people it will make everyone nervous.

Mr. Kourchenko: Exactly! We have to send the message to the others that if they don't perform, they have to go. There's nothing like a bit of adrenalin to focus the mind.

Ms. McCartney: But if we get someone new, they will take a long time to get used to the company.

Mr. Kourchenko: Hmm. That's a good point. But we could always promote someone from inside the company.

Ms. McCartney: But what about poor Jim? He's 56. Where is he going to find a new job at his age?

Mr. Kourchenko: We can offer him early retirement. I'm sure he will be happy to take a big redundancy package and spend the rest of his years on the golf course. Anything else?

Ms. McCartney: No, not really.

Mr. Kourchenko: OK, so let's summarize the points. You Begin . . .

Lesson 5

CD T-17

Mr. Kourchenko: Now that we're on the right track and have started to come out of the slump, we need to monitor our processes very closely and work on continuous improvement to avoid getting into trouble. Ms. Edwards . . .

Ms. Edwards: Yes, sir.

Mr. Kourchenko: I want you to assess our progress in the sales department in the last two trimesters of the year.

Ms. Edwards: The last two trimesters ? Will do.

Mr. Kourchenko: Yes. You will analyze and compare all the sales figures... Can you start tomorrow on this?

Ms. Edwards: Tomorrow? Let's see. Tomorrow is October 3rd. Sure, no problem. When do you need the report?

Mr. Kourchenko: Umm, okay. Tomorrow is the 3rd. U-huh, I'll need the report on my desk by October 14th.

Ms. Edwards: October 14th. No problem, sir. You'll have my report on time.

Mr. Kourchenko: Thank you, Ms. Edwards. And now let's see, Mr. Shibuya, in your case I need you to design a new training program that includes the new systems we have established. This training program will be for new employees in the production department.

Mr. Shibuya: Sure, no problem sir.

Mr. Kourchenko: Okay, and . . . Well, decide on the number of hours that will be needed and organize the sessions in a two-week period. That's possible, isn't it?

Mr. Shibuya: It is. No problem sir.

Mr. Kourchenko: Okay then. So I want you to start tomorrow as well. This program is due in three weeks time, okay?

Mr. Shibuya: Okay, sir. No problem.

Mr. Kourchenko: OK. That's it for now. Thank you, both, for your time and keep up the good work.

Mr. Shibuya and Ms. Edwards: Thank you, sir.

Lesson 6

CD T-18

Mr. Kourchenko: Well, I guess you both know the reason why we're here today; we need a manager for the marketing department to replace Jim Webber. I needed to talk to both of you because I personally think that this opening is a great chance to promote someone within the company. I would not like to hire someone from outside at this time because that person would not be familiar with our current situation and would not be familiar with our systems and our standards.

Ms. Edwards: Do you have someone in mind?

Mr. Kourchenko: As a matter of fact I do Ms. Edwards. I have three people in mind: A. J. Bundy, Sarah E. Mackenzie and Krista Higgins. Here you have a copy of their files. I want to take both of your opinions into consideration for this decision.

Ms. Edwards: Is there any specific profile you're looking for?

Mr. Kourchenko: Well, as you know, Marketing is not an easy area to work in. The candidate must know the market well and have great intuition and people skills. Another important characteristic is dedication, enough persistence to reach his or her objectives. And, of course this job requires patience as well.

Mr. Shibuya: Well, what about A.J. Bundy? He was best salesman of the year and I know he is very persistent.

Ms. Edwards: But look, he is still a student and he might not be able to work full time. I think we absolutely need someone with full-time availability.

Mr. Kourchenko: That's a good point. I would not want a candidate who is still studying as this is a managerial position. What could be relevant is experience. What about Sarah Mackenzie? It might be a good idea to promote someone within the company who has been here for a while and that has experience in marketing.

Ms. Edwards: Mmm, I think she could be a good candidate as she is familiar with our current situation. I mean, she already works in the marketing department.

Mr. Kourchenko: That's right, she is a very good member of the team. However, I am not sure about her age. I would prefer to have someone younger who will not be retiring in a few years.

Mr. Shibuya: So, we have Krista Higgins left. She has an excellent profile.

Ms. Edwards: I agree. I personally think that she is the best candidate. Working in the sales department has given her enough knowledge of marketing to know it's indispensable. However, her degree is in accounting. Is that relevant?

Mr. Kourchenko: Oh, yes. You need a good head for figures if you're working in marketing. Yes, I think Krista would make excellent Marketing Manager. OK? I think we all agree that Ms. Krista Higgins is the best candidate for this opening. Thank you for your time and . . .

Unit 5   Solving problems

Lesson 1

It's Tuesday afternoon and Wayne and Mike are at work. Wayne is in the sales department and Mike is in charge of shipping and receiving at PHARMAQWIK. Wayne goes into the warehouse and asks Mike about some pharmaceutical orders.

Mike: Hey, Wayne. How's it going?

Wayne: Not too bad . . . Uhh, Mike . . . I just got a call from ARNO Medical Center. They're wondering when their order will be ready. They were supposed to get it yesterday.

Mike: Let's see, ARNO Medical Center. Here it is. They ordered 50 cases of NAPIL-50, 50 cases of NAPIL-30, and 50 cases of NAPIL-80. The reason it hasn't been shipped is that NAPIL-50 is on back order.

Wayne: Do you know when the shipment will arrive?

Mike: Yep. I just spoke to the lab and they said it's on the truck and it'll be here tomorrow. So ARNO should have theirs the day after tomorrow.

Wayne: Great. I'll let them know. Listen, I have a couple of other questions. Do you know how many drums of disinfectant we have in stock? And I also need to know how many bottles of alcohol and iodine there are. I'm working on a few orders and I'd like to avoid any back orders.

Mike: I can't tell you right now but if you give me a minute, I'll check it out for you.

Wayne: Sure. I'll be in my office. Just give me a ring.

Mike: You got it!

Lesson 3

Walter: Miss Mancuso, have you notified senior management about tomorrow's meeting?

Nicole: Yes, sir. I circulated the agenda to everyone and they've all confirmed that they can attend.

Walter: And did you tell them all to bring their list of the equipment in their departments that they think needs to be replaced?

Nicole: Just like you told me.

Walter: Good. Because that stock list is really important. Is Ana going to be writing up the minutes for us tomorrow?

Nicole: No, she's not. I'm going to do them.

Walter: No problem. Now, we need to kick off tomorrow's meeting at 10 A.M. prompt because we have a lot of things to cover on the agenda.

Nicole: Don't worry. I'll be ready. Ugh, I really hate to bring this up now, but the conference room isn't quite ready yet. They are having problems with the projector.

Walter: But will it be ready in time for the meeting? Look, I've spent a long time working on some really great diagrams. We need to get the projector fixed by tomorrow.

Nicole: Don't worry, sir. The technicians are working on it now.

Walter: Great! OK, anything we forgot?

Nicole: No, sir. I'm going to make some spare copies of our equipment inventory, just in case anyone forgets theirs. And I've ordered your favorite pastries.

Walter: Great. So we're all set.

Lesson 4

CD T-22

Presentation 1

Speaker: OK, everyone. Can you all see? Great. Now let's start by looking at the horizontal axis. Clearly this shows the years going back to 1998. The vertical axis shows the percentage of market share divided between ourselves and our major competitors. As you can see, our market share has decreased dramatically whereas theirs has steadily increased.

Presentation 2

Speaker: Good morning everyone! To begin my presentation, I would like to show you the following diagram which shows the chain of command in our company. Firstly, at the top of the pecking order is the CEO. Her subordinates - at the next level down - are the department managers.

Presentation 3

Speaker: Morning guys. We've started work on some systems to help you streamline general repairs and maintenance of equipment. Now, can we look at the first diagram? First off, some terms. The rectangles . . . these boxes are called process boxes, think ACTION, and when you see one of these you have to do something. The diamond shaped boxes are called decision boxes and obviously, this is the point in the process where you have to make a decision. So when you get to this stage, stop and THINK or ASK your immediate supervisor . . .

Presentation 4

Speaker: Can you all see this diagram? Fine. Now, we can start anywhere on the diagram. That's the point - it's like a circle? - one thing leads to another and you return to the same point. Let's start at "Increased Sales". Now, if sales go up, then so do profits which in turn leads to an increase in investment in research and development. This will then result in a better product and so we return to the beginning with increased sales.

Presentation 5

Speaker: . . . Now, let's look at this diagram that I've prepared. The three circles represent the three groups of people that concern us and, as you can see, the circles overlap. This is where one group interacts with another group. So, clearly, teachers and students interact at school. The big question I have for you today is what happens when all three circles coincide? Are we bringing all three groups together? I'd like you to think about that.

Presentation 6

Speaker: . . . Now let's turn to the next diagram. Let's start at the top - the apex- the most important part of our business - customer confidence. But how do we achieve good customer confidence? As you can see this is based on trust. No trust - no confidence. But what is the foundation of trust? Clearly, it is service. Customer service is the base of all our activities.

Lesson 5

CD T-23

Walter: Ladies and gentlemen. Nice to see you all here. We're a little short on time so we'd better get down to business. A lot of our equipment is getting old so, our first objective is to prioritize which equipment needs to be replaced. Secondly, our market share has fallen over the past four months and thirdly, we have a very serious legal matter on our hands which I'd like Vincent de Nero to go over. If there is any other outstanding business, we'll address it at the end, please.

Now our first point, we have 30 minutes to prioritize which equipment to replace. Jim, would you mind telling us what the priorities are in Radiography.

Jim: Sure. There is a great new scanner that has just come on to the market. We have to keep the department up-to-date, and I feel as though we need to buy one.

Walter: Fine, Jim, but I think you are missing the point. We are trying to identify old equipment that needs replacing.

Jim: Right! OK, the OPG machine is about 20 years old and is very unreliable. We are having to spend a lot of money on maintenance and half the time it doesn't work.

Walter: OK, so would you mind letting me know what it would cost to replace it, and send me three quotes by, let's say, next Friday. Now, Karen.

Karen: Thanks, Walter. OK, we're having a lot of problems with our Internet server. It seems our FWT computer terminals are not entirely compatible with their WSST language protocol. We're getting a lot of conflict error codes in the log.

Walter: So, what you are trying to say is that we either change the server or buy new computers.

Karen: Yeah. That's a pretty good summary.

Lesson 6

CD T-24

Conversation 1

Manager: What do you mean you're quitting!!!!

Employee: Yup.

Manager: You can't leave like that!! I need time to find a replacement.

Employee: You know. . . That's your problem. It's not my worry.

Manager: Why didn't you give any notice!!!

Employee: Hey. Something suddenly came up. Gotta go with the flow.

Conversation 2

Manager: Well, I'm very sorry to hear that you're leaving.

Employee: Yeah, me too. But it's time to move on. I hope you can find my replacement in the next two weeks. I'll be happy to help you train my replacement if you find someone soon.

Manager: Thank you. I'll take you up on your offer, and thanks for being professional.

Lesson 6

CD T-25

Walter: Vincent, I'd like you to address our third issue on the agenda.

Vincent: The reason I was asked to attend this meeting was to inform you about an imminent lawsuit.

All: What?

Vincent: One of our patients that was receiving treatment here was given the wrong medication and nearly died. Luckily, he is expected to fully recover.

However, the family, after receiving legal advice, has filed a malpractice lawsuit against us. We have already spoken to the physician who prescribed the medication and the nurse who administered it.

Committee member A: But what happened? Was it an allergic reaction?

Vincent: It's still under investigation, but it appears to have been negligence.

Committee member A: Oh my god!! What does that mean?

Vincent: It means we're still investigating, but the negligence was not on our part. It seems our supplier, PHARMAQWIK, sent us some NAPIL - 30 that in reality was NAPIL - 80.

Committee member B: You mean they put the medicine in the wrong bottle?

Vincent: Actually, it was in the right bottle.

Committee member A: Well, I'm really confused.

VINCENT: Hold on a sec. Somehow the labels on the medicine bottles were damaged or altered. and PHARMAQWIK's shipping clerk sent the bottles with water damaged labels. Here, look at the picture. Do you see how half of the number eight looks like a three?

All: Yeah. Yes.

Vincent: Well, this little mistake, or should I say HUGE mistake, was the reason for the patient's overdose. The doctor prescribed NAPIL-30, and Jenny Merton, one of our nurses mistakenly gave the patient 80 mg. instead of 30mg. She never imagined the dose was wrong because the label said 30 when in reality it was 80. So, we're preparing all the documents that we'll need for the suit against PHARMAQWIK.

Committee member B: Was the medication checked here? I mean, Gerry, the warehouse guy, inspects all the medication we receive.

Vincent: Well, that's a good question, but . . .